WELCOMING
SPIRIT HOME

TO: Nancy,

May the incoming
spirit bring you much
love, joy and inspiration
May you be always

blessed -

Sobonfu

FOREWORD

A child is born. S/he comes into the world of nature, perhaps in a simple structure where bird song can be heard. The breath of life is blown into her nostrils by the midwife, and the child draws into herself this new world. A loving and supportive embrace of mother and family surrounds her from the first moment — there are more people who want to hold her than there are hours in the day. She hears the singing of women as they work around the lodges; she hears the singing of men in the fields or forest. The people around her in the community know how to get along well, and she learns these ways of relationship with ease. Love fills her days before she has a word for it.

Often she is with her grandparents and other elders who share the stories of her family and the wisdom of her people. She grows up never knowing what separation means. She runs, plays, and explores among the living things around her, while the old ones tell her what they are — a healing plant, a herd animal, a bird of great beauty. Her elders watch her and give her a tantalizing array of experiences and choices, so that her natural tendencies and gifts begin to show themselves. They look deeply into her spirit with their wise, Spirit-filled eyes. What she loves and who she is becomes clearly evident, and the uniqueness of her contribution to the people is seen and named and nurtured. The only code of the village is to support the highest intention and finest being of each person. Spirit is honored in the child and in all things. She becomes masterful at what she loves, and offers a great gift to her people, from her heart through her hands.

A child is born. S/he comes into glaring brightness in a room with no windows, surrounded by the smell of chemicals. Her basic instinct is to be frightened, for her mother's heart-beat has changed and the baby senses her stress. When she has passed through that challenging canal into the light of her own day, she is taken from her mother when she most needs the assurance of lying on that familiar heartbeat. Something stings her eyes. She is alone. Her crying brings no response, and she finally falls into an exhausted sleep, to wake up again alone in a crib. When she finally goes home with her mother, she is still alone much of the time. Her mother is alone and often exhausted, overwhelmed with caring for her and the rest of the family. There is no one there to help her.

Before very long, the baby is left all day in a strange place with a stranger who is busy with many other stressed and cry-ing children. She adjusts. She draws into herself in a certain way. Her wishes feel like demands that are not being met, and hurt and anger enter before she has words for them. No one

WELCOMING SPIRIT HOME

ANCIENT AFRICAN TEACHINGS
TO CELEBRATE CHILDREN AND COMMUNITY

SOBONFU E. SOMÉ

Author of *The Spirit of Intimacy*

NEW WORLD LIBRARY
NOVATO, CALIFORNIA

New World Library
14 Pamaron Way
Novato, CA 94949

Copyright © 1999 by Sobonfu E. Somé
Editorial: Becky Benenate
Cover design: Alexandra Honig

Library of Congress Cataloging-in-Publication Data

Somé, Sobonfu.
Welcoming spirit home : ancient african teachings to celebrate
children and community
Sobonfu E. Somé
p.   cm.
ISBN 1-57731-009-8 (alk. paper)
1. Parenting — Religious aspects. 2. Dagari (African people)
— Burkino Faso — Religion.   I. Title.
BL625.8.S55   1999
299'.64—dc21
98-42952
CIP

First printing, September 1999
ISBN 1-57731-009-8
Printed in U.S.A. on acid-free paper
Distributed to the trade by Publishers Group West

10 9 8 7 6 5 4 3 2

This book is dedicated to all the children around the world. May you continue to carry within you the divine blessings. May life smile on you. May your purpose remain alive and enrich and heal our lives. May you find in this world a strong foundation and a source of empowerment.

CONTENTS

has time to watch her closely, to give her attention and individual experiences, to watch her response, to let her show what she loves. Home at night is full of tired people, still busy with chores at home after a long day of work. Television entertains her. Finally the whole family is together — around the TV, where someone else's life or fiction or violence is being portrayed. None of the family stories or wisdom have been given her, and she grows up not knowing who she is.

An adult has to drive her everywhere she goes, down busy streets and highways, and she is frightened to go outside alone. In school, she is asked to sit still, to be quiet, to control her natural tendencies and interests — her aliveness is dampened into obedience. She is molded to the structure around her, made to be a good little worker. Her rhythm is tuned to someone else's needs. A bell rings and she has a small taste of freedom. Then back to her seat. She tries to pick some job she would like to do in her life. It doesn't work out so well, because her days are deadened and dull. Loud music and stimulants — coffee and then stronger things — help sometimes, but not for long. Sometimes she can't even relax at night, and must take something to quiet herself and the dull ache in her head.

Which one of these is more like your early years? And your children's? Which one do you want for your children, and the children to come? Which community would you like to call your home?

This book will help you make choices that can move you

more closely toward creating a community of spirit, even today, even in our modern world.

I had the joy and privilege of spending time with Sobonfu Somé at our recent "Confluence," where she and Malidoma Patrice Somé sat with me on the council as we worked together with a large group of participants. I was very impressed by her exuberant nature, her childlike clarity and innocent perception, her willingness to speak her truth without judgment, as well as the depth of her knowing. As she and Malidoma spoke to us about the Dagara way of working with the ancestors, and then led us in a simple ritual, I experienced a deep sense of the power of primary ways, which we in this world have largely lost. It made me yearn for more, and so I was thrilled to receive this wonderful book that helps guide us in using the sacred more effectively in our lives.

So many current events, including the violence in our children's schools, tell us clearly that we must pay more loving attention to our children, and to the community in which they are raised. No longer can we delude ourselves that a "prosperous" home, a "good" school, a "community" of non-relating individuals, and the TV can assure our children's future. The way we live our lives is filled with loss — we are losing our greatest asset in not devoting ourselves to our upcoming generations; we are losing the true joy of life in having no real community; and we are losing tremendous help for our daily lives when we forget our ancestors. We are deadened by the lack of Spirit in our lives. We are at a loss.

In my own heart, and in my interactions with people all around the world, I sense a longing, a searching for some basic happiness that eludes us. Whether or not we can articulate it, we are longing for this larger on-going community — from our ancestors before us, through the community where Sobonfu reminds us we "can find a home in each other's heart and soul," and on into the generations of children who come after us. Without it, we are not truly human. We have lost our greatest treasure, our true humanity.

When we look deeply into ourselves and into who we are as a species, we must perceive ourselves to be a people of extended family and clan, living within larger communities of shared wisdom and abilities. To live as we live today — separated into nuclear families who sometimes do not even spend time with each other — is to deny the finest and most joyful aspects of ourselves. Some strange part of our mind tells us that if we just work harder, if we just have a little (or a lot) more money, if we just make it to retirement, if we just (fill in your own blanks!) then everything will be all right. Yet we must soon confront the fact that this has nothing to do with the truth. It has much to do with being part of the large corporate machine, but little to do with what really works for us, little to do with our hearts, little to do with our sweet and lovely humanity.

The real answer to most of our challenges is to choose to

take the time to regain the essential qualities of our lives that we so yearn for — the wholeness and holiness that is ours to reclaim — and to bring Spirit full and radiant into the guidance of our daily steps.

May this book of wisdom from a powerful and primary woman inform your days with beauty and prosperity.

> — Brooke Medicine Eagle
> Flathead Valley, Montana
> The eve of the millennium

ACKNOWLEDGMENTS

To N'nan and all my mothers. To Borbiè-Luonmuon and all my fathers. To my grandparents and those who have gone before me. To my sisters, nieces, nephews, and all the children in my life. You have all taught me how to love and be loved. You have made me the person I am today. My heart remains forever with you.

To Becky Benenate, my editor. Words are lacking in how to say thank you to you. Your dedication to my ancestors' wisdom and the diligence with which you worked on this book have turned my thoughts into a comprehensible and readable book. From the depth of my heart, thank you.

To all of you who have given me the push to finish this book and to all those who have worked in the background, my sincere thanks. *Ye Barka!*

INTRODUCTION

My name is Sobonfu Somé, which means "keeper of the rituals, keeper of knowledge." I came to this country from Burkina Faso in West Africa. Burkina Faso means "the land of the Proud Ancestors" in the African language.

I have been working for many years to bring the ways of my people to other parts of the world. As my name suggests, I bring the mysteries of the old ways — the rituals — to our people and other people around the world to help them go through life's continuous changes.

Although I currently live in the West most of the year, I still practice native rituals and consider my spirit closely tied to Burkina Faso and the Dagara tribe. Through my work, I bring rituals to the West to help people grow toward authentic spiritual enrichment.

This book focuses on the wisdom of my ancestors in celebrating childbirth, children, healing, community, and the rituals we honor among our tribe. It is my way of bringing to the West the kinds of spiritual blessings we have in our village in Africa.

⊷⇒◉⇐⊷

As we start on this journey, I feel it would be helpful to share with you a little background about our country, our village, and the ways of our people.

Burkina Faso is about the size of Colorado. I don't know how many millions of people are there now — about eight or nine — it's hard to say because we don't count people. It is a very simple country. In fact, it is almost impossible to find any documented information on it. The most readily available information are the many warnings issued by the World Health Organization that depict Burkina Faso as the capital for many dangerous illnesses, with malaria at the top of its list. Aside from the few sad wild animals trapped inside two parks for tourists to see, Burkina Faso, as a land-locked country, does not have anything substantial to offer tourists — except the generosity, kindness, spirituality, and hospitality of its people.

In Africa, Burkina Faso is known as the home for West Africa's culture with its promotion of arts, crafts, films, and cultural diversity. If you go to Burkina Faso, the combination of its hidden values and simple magic make you feel welcome and at home. This is largely what makes Burkina Faso different from other sub-Saharan countries.

It is a diverse country. There are approximately sixty tribes in Burkina Faso, with as many languages and cultures. The northern part is desert — the Sahara. The central part is flat, and the southern part is hilly, grassy, and a bit green. The soil mixture varies from place to place, but the common red soil, resembling that of Georgia, contrasts beautifully with our few trees. We have two seasons, one rainy and one dry. The poor condition of the roads — with holes, dust, and mud — is made worse by these seasons, so traveling is difficult.

Burkina Faso is what you would call a savanna type of land, mostly dry grassland with few trees taller than 30 feet. The tallest trees are the African mahogany (*kaya senegalensis*), a tree called *gaa* in Dagara (*diospyros mespiliformis*), and the famous baobab tree (*adansonia digitata*). These trees can grow up to 180 feet. The gradual desert condition has replaced the old forestlike environment with bushes, although here and there you might see some dense groves of trees such as the *shea* (*butyrospermum parkii*), which is known for its healing power, cosmetics, and cooking values.

⇥⟨≣⟩⇤

Looking at my village with a Western eye, one could say that the poverty is unbelievable. It is the same in my village as in most African villages. What people do not see, however, is the spiritual richness amidst the poverty. It is this spiritual unity and the simplicity of life that help people to live in a healthy and happy way. Wealth is not determined by how much we have in our bank accounts but by how many people we have around us and how much our spirit, soul, and heart have to offer.

People of my heritage don't understand when I explain to them that I have many "things," that I have material objects. One time I took pictures of all the things in my apartment and brought them home for people to look at. They just shook their heads in confusion. They didn't understand why I would surround myself with so much "stuff."

The elders see collecting material objects as a way of actually keeping yourself away from spirit, of "stuffing" yourself until there is no more room for spirit. When this happens spirit could be at your door knocking and you can't answer it — there is no room.

In Western culture many people have a great deal of material wealth yet still feel an emptiness that constantly reminds them something is missing in their lives. Many search for happiness throughout their entire lives. The idea of pursuing happiness is an ironic one to me. No one ever said to me, "I have pursued happiness and I found it." It seems to me that each time you say "I am one inch away" and you are about to put your hand on it, it is a thousand miles away and you have to run after it again. It becomes a continual chase.

I can feel the effect of modernity within my life. I can feel the difference between being in California, where life is complex, and being in Africa, where life is very simple. In Africa I don't need to worry about doing the carpet, or doing *anything*, for that matter. I am happier there than I am here. Here it is easy to lose, or forget, myself — I have to catch an airplane, I have a schedule to keep. It's one thing after another, and there is no end to it. I find myself really trying to make sure that I don't become devoured by this material world, and I strive to stay focused with life as I used to live it.

The only way I keep my sanity here is through ritual — constantly doing ritual. I feel grateful that I have a park outside the back of my apartment where I can go and truly be with nature, be with the earth. I can let the earth support me and simply voice my concern about my daily life to the nature spirit, to the earth. My greatest fear is losing the identity I have when I am in Africa. Just voicing my concerns to the spirit has been very helpful to me.

When I get on a plane and fly to various places, I especially notice how differently I feel. I must be able to do ritual daily to keep myself grounded; otherwise I start to fly around and get lost in all those thoughts and all those things to do.

--=◉◎=--

The Dagara people are socially or communally not that different from indigenous communities elsewhere. We don't have the conveniences or modern amenities one has in the West, such as electricity or running water. Nor do we live in houses without bugs. We are very close to the earth and to nature. In the village, life is directly inspired by the earth, by the trees, by the hills and rivers, and the kind of relationship that exists between people and nature is directly translated in subtle ways in the building of the community and in the relationships that exist among people. This is the gift we receive from such a place.

The Dagara people live together in large families. Our houses are compounds made of earth mixed with grass and supported by wood poles. The houses are always built in a circle, one against the other, until there is no more room to add another. Only then does it become necessary to begin a new compound. It is inside this compound that a family, made of dozens of people, lives. In reality, we only sleep inside the compounds, because life is lived outside most of the time, and there is a complete immersion into the natural world. Dagara people are known for their spiritual practices and their visionary ability. We live at the threshold between the ancestor world — the world of spirit — and the human world.

Our worldview involves five elements: fire, water, earth, mineral, and nature. Each element is understood in a very broad sense.

Fire is about dreaming, passion, keeping our connection to the ancestors, and keeping our visions alive.

Water is peace, focus, wisdom, and reconciliation.

Earth elements are responsible for our sense of identity, and our ability to nurture, to be grounded, and to support one another.

Mineral elements help us to remember our purpose and give us the means to communicate and to make sense out of what others are saying. It is the element that brings people together.

Nature helps us to be our true selves, to go through major changes and life-threatening situations. It brings magic and laughter. It takes our masks off. It is the element of transmutation, changing from one state of being or stage to another, just like a butterfly changes from a caterpillar into a cocoon and finally into a butterfly.

All these elements are embodied in both the human constitution and in our system of rituals that allow us to function in a harmonious and balanced way. The lack or the imbalance of one of these elements can create a state of crisis in our lives, and ritual is needed to bring back the balance.

WHAT IS RITUAL?

Before we continue, the term "ritual" needs a deeper understanding. Most people understand ritual as a kind of activity repeated over and over where some people perform the activity and others are spectators. Often ritual is seen as some kind of activity that people performed centuries ago that no longer has meaning and value. When ritual is connected to indigenous spirituality, people often react negatively to it because it is something they don't understand, and is out of their comfort zone. And, to make things worse, most rituals portrayed on television are often seen as negative, abusive, and ridiculous. There is a difference, however, between what the media often portray and what ritual actually is. The kinds of rituals I describe in this book have nothing to do with devil worship or satanic practices. Dagara rituals are about healing, acknowledgment of people and their gifts, and making spirit visible or tangible.

A ritual is a ceremony in which we call in spirit to be the driving force, the overseer of our activities. It is a way for us to find our way to wholeness, peace, self-acceptance, and acceptance of others. Ritual allows us to connect with the self, the community, and the natural forces around us. Ritual helps us to remove blocks between us and our true spirit.

The purpose of rituals is to take us to a place of self-discovery and mastery. In this sense ritual is to the soul what food is to the physical body. When we understand the full meaning of rituals and their importance, we can put our suspicions to rest. There are countless rituals in Africa, with many variations depending on family and tribes. The important thing to consider when doing a ritual is our intention and purpose for doing it. For without a clear intention and purpose, the ritual has no meaning.

When participating in rituals, one must leave the "Hollywood" mentality behind, for this kind of thinking turns people into spectators, and spectators kill the power of the ritual. Rituals are participatory activities that involve the whole being: body, spirit, mind, and soul. In our rituals, we call in spirits, ancestors, and dimensional beings to guide us each step of the way. Rituals are a form of continuous prayer. They help us to consciously incorporate healthy, genuine spiritual evolution and to dwell in the sacred in a way that truly heals us. For example, if you are experiencing some kind of blockage in life, you may need a fire ritual to help you remove the block and stay connected to the ancestors and keep your vision alive. You may also need a water ritual to help you stay focused.

Throughout the book I give examples of how ritual is used in our daily lives to honor and celebrate childbirth, children, and community. Through this system of ritual we come to understand the interconnectedness of spirit, community, children, and the ancestors — how they come together and how one cannot survive without another. As I share stories of the ancient ways, you will discover how, in your own ways, you, too, can live with rituals.

In our village we have been doing these rituals for thousands of years, and they are deeply ingrained within our daily lives. We use the power of that awareness in everyday life. My hope is that as you read through these pages, you will allow your indigenous self to come alive, and you will reawaken the part of you that understands the language of spirit and ritual as well as its deep meaning and healing effects. In so doing you will be able to apply the power, understanding, and completeness you gain from these rituals to your everyday life in order to be more contented, fulfilled, and complete. You can then expand this knowledge to your community and gain a deep sense of purpose and peace.

Ritual is not limited to just indigenous people; it is the

language of spirit, and has a universal dimension to it.

May the power and strength of the ancestors be a guiding light for you.

COMMUNITY

In the village, community life is built upon spirit. We know that spirit is constantly present. Spirit brings us clarity, provides inspiration, allows peace, and gives us all the blessings we need. In a sense, spirit is so incorporated in the fabric of community that it is impossible to disassociate the two. The presence of spirit in community makes it possible for the community to be the guiding light of the tribe.

WHAT IS COMMUNITY?

To better understand the term "community," it may be easier to begin by explaining what community is not. Community is not a place where you can stay without having a sense of who is around, nor is it an item on the market for sale. Rather, a community is an environment where you can find a home in each other's heart and soul. It is a living entity with spirit as its anchor, where a group of people are empowered by one another, by spirit, and by the ancestors to be themselves, carry out their purpose, and use their power responsibly. Without all these elements, community suffers from power struggles, irresponsibility, and lack of accountability.

Although there are no police to make sure people are applying these elements to their lives, everyone lives by one's own rules and the rules of spirit: the rules of integrity, honor, and responsibility toward spirit first and toward one another second. We cannot afford not to trust someone in the village. The rule of thumb is to trust people first unless they show you otherwise. This is why we do not have contracts with one another or live in fear that others will falter.

I must say that having been raised under the "trust everyone" concept brought me many painful, although good, lessons when I first started to live in the United States. Although no one is perfect, in today's world in places where the sense of community has vanished, people too often think that humans are by nature bad, or even worse, evil. This unconscious suspicion makes it impossible for people to get close to one another — not to mention build a community. We become intolerant of others simply because they remind us too much of our own flaws. We are scared of being betrayed because we have betrayed others and have been let down too many times.

To build community we must learn to go beyond these cultural prisons and perceptions. We must make an effort to heal our wounded self so it does not stand in our way of creating community. We can learn a great deal from the way Mother Earth holds us all — the criminals, the saints, the weak, the strong, the rich, and the poor — without rejecting us, and always giving us a chance to start over.

The goal of community is to form a diverse body of people with common goals and empower them to embrace their own gifts, selves, and nature. Community holds a space for all its members to work at becoming as close to their true selves as possible.

SPIRIT IS A PART OF US

In my village we do not feel we need solitude. We can have our personal time while we are talking to somebody else. We can have our meditation time while we are in the community context. There is no need to be separated from the group to have solitude. Solitude already exists within the group — it's a part of the whole. When we start to divide or separate it means that something in the whole is not working for us. Because we have permission to be ourselves within the community, we have no need for solitude.

Because spirit is a continuous part of each of us, it is not necessary for us to take time out to sit quietly and meditate to get close to spirit. Spirit is always with us.

It is common, in my country, to see two people talking and then, simultaneously, pause. In that pause many things can be happening. They can be meditating, or they can be having personal time to "tune in." But people will never say, "I have to go be alone." It's a foreign concept — it just doesn't fit.

If you say you need to be alone in our village, people will wonder, "What is it that is not working for you that you have to be alone? What is happening that I should know to support you?"

⊸═◉═⊷

A changing Africa has brought a lot of pressure in the life of our people. Every year when I return home I find that a new aspect of modern life has been brought into the village. However, many things such as family, community, and leadership structure remain the same.

We don't have a leader or chief whom everybody follows. Instead of leaders, our guides are spirit and the ancestors. This is difficult for many people to understand, but the lives of everyone in our community are built upon the foundation given to us by spirit and the ancestors. This forces us not only to be our own police but also to take responsibility and to be accountable. It is not up to an individual to take care of someone's wrongdoing; rather, it is up to the spirit and the ancestors. And, because we don't like reporting to these forces, we make sure we don't fall into our own traps.

When conflict does arise, people do not run away or move to a new community. They see the conflict as a timely gift sent by spirit to clear obstructions in their lives. Conflict is a way to boost closeness in their intimate lives with others. Without conflict to crack open hidden thoughts, meanings, and energies, and without the means of dealing with conflict, a community is bound to stagnate and eventually cease to exist. Conflict, in a sense, is the barometer of a community. The way we deal with conflict tells us about our state of maturity and where we are as individuals as well as community.

The ruling forces that exist in the Dagara tribe are spirit and the ancestors, because they are able to see past, present, and future, and because they are able to be impartial at all times. Human beings are subject to judgments, influences, and mind changes; ancestors or spirits are not. An individual who has committed a crime will most certainly be put in the spotlight by the ancestors. This happens, for instance, when a person is seen by a *diviner* (a person who sees past, present, and future; a holy person), and the ancestors expose the crime to the diviner. It is then the *diviner's* role to let the person know that the diviner also knows about the crime. It is not, however, the diviner's responsibility to "punish" the person for the criminal act. If the individual seeks the help of the village, the village will make itself available to the individual. In the event the criminal refuses to admit what happened, the village will then turn the matter over to spirit and the ancestors. This way of dealing with matters, because it does not have a human-based justice system or any kind of hierarchy within the system, is often looked upon by anthropologists as a primitive way of leadership.

CONTRIBUTING TO THE WHOLE

The community concept is based on the fact that each person is invaluable and truly irreplaceable. Each person has a gift to give, a contribution to make to the whole. The kind of gift a person brings, the kind of being a person is, is very unique to him or her and is valued by the community. The community is constantly affirming each person, and that constant affirmation is why people are always in the community. We sleep together. We work together. We walk together. When we are "separate" we are vulnerable and are more likely to underestimate the self. This way of life may sound like an invasion of privacy to a lot of people, but not in my village. Being in a community forces us to cultivate a deeper sense of intimacy with one another, to notice one another and value one another's gifts.

Community provides a safe container in which individuals can bring their gifts. Community is also like a marketplace where individuals know they can offer their gifts, and they will be received by people who need and value them, while they also are able to receive others' gifts and talents. The spirit of community is like a big home in which all its members can find a sense of belonging. For community to work it takes the commitment, dedication, and input of all involved. It must be based on spirit as its main guide and driving force.

I know that the concept of community with spirit as its guide may be difficult to understand. As you continue to read this book, however, you will discover a deeper understanding of how to incorporate this concept into your own life and community.

In recent times, the word "community" has been misused and battered, so it does not always bring positive connotations. Many people in Western society experience community as an entity that deprives and invalidates them rather than supporting and validating them. However, the energy that invalidates self, spirit, and others is always present in a place that lacks community. I can see places in Africa that are becoming modernized where this invalidating energy is present, because they have become disconnected from community, spirit, and their ancestors. For example, in my village people are happy when someone receives something because everyone knows it can be used or shared by the whole community, whereas in some cities and villages there is beginning to be a sense of jealousy surrounding the material — people do not want others to have more than they have.

Coveting things, and even the awareness and recognition of who has more than others, have strong potential to destroy community. What is frightening for me is that as the elders die, the old ways tend to die with them. This is why they say in Africa, "When an elder dies it's like a whole library has burned down." All the wisdom and knowledge goes with that person.

When I go back to Africa I don't stay in the cities and talk about my experiences in the United States. I go back to the village to be with the old ways, because the village is where life happens and where my community welcomes me home.

There have been attempts to educate our youth about the

danger of losing community. Many people from the West who have experienced the kind of damage and destruction invalidating energy can do to a community have joined our elders in the process of educating our youth.

When you go to the cities of Africa and you inquire about going to the villages, many people, especially young people, are baffled at the idea of Westerners wanting to be associated with what they call "deep Africa." They look at you as if you are crazy. For them it is incomprehensible that a person who was born and raised in a city in the modern world would want to abuse themselves with the mediocre kind of life that one has in a village. They understand that education and schooling is a means of learning to forget about Africa and its community lifestyle, including everything involved with it.

There are people who were not born in Africa — and who are not of African descent — who are far more African than some people who were born and raised in Africa. It is an irony, because so many Africans are now negating the whole African culture while many others want to be immersed in it.

In the past few years, however, I have started to meet many Africans who live abroad and who have reached dead ends. They have experienced deep grief about having lost everything in their search for the Western ways. They now seek to go back to the old traditional ways. But the way back is not always an easy journey, especially when they are looking for a quick fix or are so desperate for change that each day that goes by feels like an eternity. It is important when waking up to the loss of community that we learn to be patient, and to be grateful that we are able to tell the difference. Only then can we take steps toward building a community without frustration.

CREATING A SENSE OF COMMUNITY

Community is the spirit, the guiding light of the tribe, whereby people come together to fulfill a specific purpose, to help others fulfill their purpose, and to take care of one another. The goal of community is to make sure that each member is heard and is properly giving the gifts he or she has brought to this world. Without this giving, community dies. And without community, individuals are left without a place where they can contribute. Community is that grounding place where people share their gifts and receive from others.

Community, as it is known in my village, cannot be replicated in the West. Here, I may never have the kind of community I had in Africa, but at least I can have a sense of it by allowing friends to be a part of what I am doing. Fifteen minutes of communication with others can help in a deep way to make up for a lack of community.

It is also possible to create a sense of community in modern societies and deepen relationships with one another through ritual. Ritual gives us the means to create a place where we can experience a sense of community with a group of people we trust and can count on with spirit's blessings; through ritual we can create a community that does not limit itself to immediate geography. Even in Africa, where community members live close to one another, we have an immediate community, the village, and the bigger community, the tribe, which encompasses tribal community members who may live far away. Tribal boundaries can cover hundreds of kilometers. For instance, the Dagara land from north to south is approximately 150 kilometers. Although the person living at the northern tip does not see the other at the southern end every day, important family matters create many occasions to bring them together.

Tribal people, even living under the pressure of modernity, do not live the kind of lifestyle people in modern cities do, and therefore the sense of community in these two places will always be inherently different. People who live outside a tribal community can draw a great deal of strength, knowledge, and support from tribal rituals and other valuable structures and activities. It would be impossible, however, to incorporate 100 percent of tribal ways into a life lived in a metropolitan city because many things are thought of in entirely different ways.

Time, for example, is thought of differently. In the village time is elastic and everyday comes with its own time, which is different from yesterdays. When someone tells you they will come by in the evening, you know that they will come over at night. You may not know the exact moment they will arrive, but it will be the right *time* when they show up.

Can you imagine explaining to your employer that your hours at work have to be flexible because you are on African time? Of course not. In the village, however, only spirit dictates what "time" things happen. Hence, life is focused on living and being present for what is around you or in front of you at any given moment.

When you become immersed in this very different kind of time energy, you can understand how tribal people are able to build a strong and deep relationship with their environment, and why a tribal person's life is focused around rituals that involve the natural environment such as the earth, rivers, mountains, trees, and rocks.

EVERYDAY LIFE THE DAGARA WAY

For the Dagara people, everyday life is predominantly lived outside the house. The moment you wake up you put all your bedding away and then you are off to greet and be greeted by the sun, the birds, the Earth, and all of nature. Afterward you go around and inquire about everyone's health and night's sleep.

One important use for the house is a place to keep shrines. One such shrine is the ancestral shrine, where daily prayers and offerings are made. It is usually made of old things like masks or an image of a long-gone ancestor, along with all kinds of meaningful things representing the ancestral world.

Life is very simple in this setting, yet very soothing and soul nourishing, brought about by the community's determination to find value in its members and to seek their gifts. It is the community's role to put each individual in the spotlight and provide him or her with a sense of home, a sense of belonging. The goal of the community is to continuously align itself with spirit, the ancestors, and everything around its surroundings. The constant concern about the health and wellbeing of its members leads a community to be highly aware of both its elders and its children. This is very important to the community because a good relationship between the very old and the very young creates a sane, healthy environment and an anchoring force for all in the village. This force makes it possible for adults to feel grounded and supported enough to fulfill their life purpose.

There is such a solid relationship among generations that children are free to roam around the village with the knowledge that they will be taken care of, that someone will always be there to hear them or to witness their experiences. The children know they are not identified solely with their parents, but they have a whole village and tribe within which they can have many mothers and fathers. This is an invaluable and irreplaceable gift — they are made to truly feel a part of a community, and are valued and cared for by many.

It is this kind of magic you find within community. This is where the often-heard phrase "It takes a whole village to raise a child" comes from. In this setting everyday life occurs: a man and a woman undergo a marriage ritual, children are born and raised within the community, and the cycle continues.

⋆═◉═⋆

BIRTH

At the heart of a healthy community lies the importance of spirit, elders, children, ritual, gift giving, ancestors, responsibility, and accountability. These fundamentals must be understood and valued, and they must be nurtured and balanced for the well-being of the community. In Africa it is known that elders are the vision and wisdom keepers, children ensure the survival of the villages and tribe, and rituals feed the soul.

⊶≡◉≡⊷

Let's begin with the miracle of birth, its place in community, how community supports the birthing process, and how the birth of a child continues the existence of community.

Life is full of many wonders that we marvel at and that keep us curious in our everyday lives. The mystery of birth is one of them. For many years scientists have been attempting to break into the mysteries surrounding pregnancy and childbirth. There have been questions and many debates about when a fetus has its own life. Some people claim that a baby has life a few months into the pregnancy; others say that a baby has life only after a live birth. Perhaps this question is the basis of the disconnection many people feel in their lifetimes. The questions that run through my mind are: What is the possibility of life before conception? And, what is the possibility of life beyond Earth?

For many indigenous people, and certainly for the Dagara people, life is not *conceived* at birth or even at conception, nor does it end after death. The reality of the Dagara starts with the assumption and the knowledge that we are able to be on Earth simply because there are forces making it possible for us to be here. These forces constantly interact with our universe and send their representatives (souls) here to bring their gifts. Without these forces, human existence would not be possible, nor would it make any sense whatsoever. If this is true, then it makes sense that our time on Earth should be spent honoring our life experiences by bringing our gifts into the world. It would also imply that we do not live just one lifetime on Earth, but that we have the possibility of coming back (having the ability to chose a particular culture, country, race, and community). It means that we are not isolated beings running aimlessly without purpose, and that our actions affect the entire universe.

OUR BIRTHRIGHT AS A CONTRACT WITH THE UNIVERSE

If we view reality from the angle that we come to Earth to fulfill a particular purpose, birth can then be looked at as a contract between this world and the world of the ancestors or other dimensions. This contract is agreed to in different ways. For some parents it is a conscious choice; for others, it is unconscious, but for the incoming soul the choice is always a conscious one. In all cases the choice to be born is welcomed by all ancestors, spirits, and community. And in this sense we are all part of one large, interwoven, community, ever growing, in this world and in worlds beyond.

We must remember that our position in respect to this contract determines the quality of life our spirits will live in our bodies. After our spirits are in human form, the difficulties of keeping the contract unaltered are always present. Some people understand these difficulties as important landmarks and are able to use them as life lessons, allowing the difficulties to remind them where to turn when they experience them. Many don't realize, however, that the circumstances we experience in our lives are things we chose — we could even say "programmed" — prior to being born. And, because of this state of ignorance or rejection of the idea that we actually plan our course, we often miss the lessons contained in the difficult experiences, and we continue to live in the dark.

If we believe that our greatest wounds are in fact our greatest gifts, we can embrace the idea that the hardships we experience in our families of origin are no accidents. Whether we are born to loving parents or abusive parents, born by natural childbirth or by Cesarean, born into or without a community, born with disabilities, or found in a trash yard, we all have unique gifts to bring to this world.

Our wounds are not only our landmarks, but our lessons —

tools from which we must learn to draw our strength and wisdom. For example, if you find yourself irritated by the lack of true community, chances are that part of the reason you chose to be born in your environment is to bring an awareness to others that community is needed for our spirit and our children's spirit to blossom.

Of course, we would like to assume that we did not have any part in such a contract so that we can blame others (such as our parents) or circumstances (such as a lack of time or affection) for our difficulties. But the truth is, we signed up for the obstacles we experience, and when we reject this truth, we spend most of our time feeling stuck and frustrated. Our spiritual growth becomes stagnant, and our gifts are not delivered to the world in a way that liberates us. As this way of life continues, our lack of spiritual growth and gift giving can turn into a toxin, a sickness that can destroy our lives.

When people do not fulfill their life purposes, they have to come back and try again, bringing different lessons to help them on their journeys. The question then becomes, How can we move forward in this life and do what we are here to do? My sense is that we start to take responsibility for signing the contract, and then find, or create, the appropriate community in which we can then deliver our gifts and be receptive to other people's gifts as well.

The understanding Dagara people have of pregnancy, birth, and the purpose of incoming souls to Earth makes them take pregnancy and the birthing process very seriously. In fact, they make sure they prepare themselves for the incoming soul in a way that allows for a healthy and welcomed arrival. This understanding is at the root of preconception, pregnancy, and afterbirth rituals.

⊷≡◐⟩⊶

Some people view the experience of giving birth as the direct translation of the happiness in their primary relationship, and therefore childbirth is an honor. Others view it as a social responsibility that takes away their personal choice; therefore, the heart finds it difficult and conflicting to deal with the incoming soul. For others still, childbirth is a burden. They do not have the desire to care for the incoming soul. For all of these people, with any and all attitudes about giving birth, ritual can provide invaluable assistance and support.

PRECONCEPTION

Most of us would go through a lot of trouble to clean or redecorate our homes in an attempt to make them beautiful if we were told that the president of the United States was coming for dinner. If the president's parents knew that the child they were going to have would someday be president of the United States, imagine what they would have done for this child — and also what everybody around this child would have done for its well-being. What would the world be like if we invested the same kind of energy into every child born? We don't always think of our children as presidents, queens, or kings who deserve clean, safe, and welcoming homes. But the fact is, they do.

For children, the equivalent of home is the womb. For this reason it is important for every couple to go on a healing journey even before they attempt to bring a child to this reality. How can we possibly save the world if we don't save our own children or change the way we deal with them?

The healing journey I speak of is one that allows a couple to take a serious look at their demons, and to reconnect with their childhood memories — if nothing else, to go through the process of realizing how vulnerable they were as children and what they can do to protect their future child and other children in the community. It is now known that each generation has the ability to heal the wounds of previous generations. We must be willing, however, to visit our old wounds to do this healing, or our children will then have to carry on those burdens. We have the capability to stop the pattern of suffering for our children; we simply need to be brave enough to take this step.

In Africa some people take a journey to the places where they were born and to the places where the placentas that once held them were buried to gather the strength to connect

44

with their past and to get in touch with their vulnerable selves and reexperience what it is like to be a child.

We heal by gathering strength from our past, from experiences that left us vulnerable and wounded. In taking a journey such as this, we learn how not to inflict the same pains on our children that we experienced.

A ritual of giving away something of value follows the healing journey, and this ritual allows room for the next ritual: the fertility ritual. In the giveaway ritual the woman wanting to have a child gives something of value, such as cloth or a basket, to another woman with a toddler. The man gives away seeds for planting crops or some cereal grains to an old woman or old man. Then, a communal giveaway is done in the form of a feast: the couple cooks a large meal and invites all the children from the village to dine with their potential sibling.

BONDING FOR A STRONG PARENTAL RELATIONSHIP

There is a spiritual dimension to every relationship, no matter what its origins and whether or not it is acknowledged as spiritual. Two people come together because spirit wants them together. What is important after the couple comes together is to look at the relationship as spirit driven instead of individual driven. When two spirits can commune and really share at the deepest level without having the minds interfere, they are bonded in a strong, sincere, and loving way.

There is a need to periodically cleanse the marriage relationship. There is always something in the self that is overcompensating, or pretending, or giving in, or pushing too hard. There is a way to become aware of these frustrating things, and overcome them — and it is through a simple ritual. By doing this simple ritual practice, all bad things the couple have accumulated are ejected.

Usually the woman sits facing north, back-to-back with the man who sits facing south, within a circle of ash. The ritual starts with an invocation of spirit. Then the two people start to express out loud, to spirit, their frustrations. As they do, their pain increases and eventually explodes — releasing the frustration and anger. Each person speaks his or her pain and and both people are able to release all their feelings.

The ritual has a powerful, emotional ending. The couple eventually slow down and then they turn to face one another and reach a reconciliation. Then they pour water onto each other, cleansing each other of the fear and pain. The heart of this process is the washing away of all the friction that has settled into the couple's life together. This ritual is not a confrontation, but rather a renewal of the marriage vow.*

When a couple bonds it makes it possible for them to be open in welcoming a new spirit into their lives.

---

* These four paragraphs are reprinted by permission from my book, *The Spirit of Intimacy*, published by William Morrow.

CLEARING THE WOMB OF POSSIBLE TOXIC ENERGY

Clearing the womb is one of the important remodeling jobs we have to do to the body's house before becoming pregnant. Without cleansing, the womb can easily become the opposite of what it was intended to be: It can become toxic. Most of us women are not always fully in touch with our feminine nature, or we have an issue with the feminine. This disconnection to the feminine creates several problems that affect our motherhood. Also, every culture has a powerful, pervasive myth that pulls and guides its people in a particular direction. Not being aware of the myth can cause you to be overwhelmed by it — even devoured by it.

Most indigenous people consider Earth their home and mother. Yet, for most people the Earth (or soil) is a dirty thing. And because the body's constitution borrows from Earth, and the womb is like fertile Earth, we often treat the womb the same way we treat Earth. If we consider Earth as a dumping ground, as something to mess with and reject, we might unconsciously treat the womb in the same way.

In many traditions, before a woman conceives she has to clear herself from whatever weakness she may feel in her femininity and amend any thoughts that may endanger the viability of the womb. In our community, a ritual "sweeping" is done to keep her from thinking or feeling negatively. With the feathers of a baby chicken and some leaves from the *gnarur* tree, her body is swept from top to bottom, and a prayer is spoken to protect her from such energy. It is only upon completion of this ritual that the calling of the child to come takes place.

FERTILITY RITUALS

Traditional indigenous cultures consider conception a sacred act and treat it as such. Because children are a gift and a blessing from the gods, the ancestors, and the great mysteries, their entry into this world must be welcomed in a sacred way.

Fertility rituals are performed to invoke the divine mysteries, to shower the couple's life with divine energy, and to bring about a constant sacred energy. These rituals are also done in many African cultures to ensure the continuation of life. They begin with acknowledging the divine energy in us and with seeking the blessings of the many divine energies around us. Some rituals start at the beginning of wedding rituals, where a prayer is performed asking the divine mysteries to bless the couple with its fertile energy. At a later time, when a couple starts to hear the call to parenthood, more rituals are done to bring about the spirit of fertility.

Fertility rituals usually take place in caves or at river banks. I recently witnessed my sister's fertility ritual. One evening she was taken to a cave behind the village. Before we started the ritual, we all gathered to pray as a way of setting our intention. A shrine to the earth and to the spirit of fertility was erected at the entrance of the cave, decorated with all kinds of child figurines, seeds, eggs, cloths, and fruits. An area used for a bed was dug out of the earth inside the cave. Then, I heard the elders and midwives explain to my sister the significance of the ritual and the meaning of each symbol on the shrine. The earth and the cave were symbolic of the womb. A big clay pot of water was symbolic of life. The eggs, seeds, and figurines were symbolic of new beginnings and new life. The elders also explained why everything on the shrine came in groups of three, four, or seven: three is the masculine number, four is the feminine, and seven is the combination of the two, which produces balance and invokes fertility. Ash was sprinkled all around the ritual space to protect it.

After a long invocation, my sister was brushed with some of the eggs, then washed and carried into the cave where she spent the night sleeping in a fetal position. We all spent the night with her, invoking songs and gently massaging her.

The cool breeze of morning reminded me that dawn was breaking. An elder motioned to carry my sister out of the cave. The elders cleared their throats and started another long prayer. We then presented my sister to the earth, the sky, and the four directions. As soon as we put my sister on the ground, I heard her voice call out,

> *Spirit of the ground I dwell upon, great ones of the open sky and you ancient ones of the earth: You walked this life before me and did it well, which is why I am alive and in your footsteps today. You*

*offered yourself to souls that came here. I'm one
of them. And today these same souls are asking
me to give myself to the sacred rite of being a
mother. They want to use the womb in me as a
sacred home to get ready for this journey to earth.
I feel blessed and I feel scared. So I ask you to
touch my pounding heart with your sacred hand
and comfort it and quiet it so I can hear the dis-
tant call of a spirit enroute to earth. Remind me
that I once made that call myself, and someone
listened, and cared for me. Teach me devotion so
I can reply with love to the call of life. Teach me
how to listen so I can feed my spirit with the food
of your instruction. Give me a shower of strength
in these times of change. Initiate me into surren-
der. I must give myself to that which is so much
greater than me.*

After my sister's prayer, a baby touched my sister's belly
with a mixture of earth and water. The elders then thanked
the ancestors and all spirits present for their participation at
the ritual. The elders understand that the language and form
of this ritual is a blessing, and also a way of calling another soul
to this world.

During this time, the husband usually participates in a similar ritual led by men so he can be *spiritually* pregnant along with
his wife. Wife and husband are united in a celebration when

they return home from their ritual. Often before conception, either during this ritual or at another time, women will hear their children calling to them and introducing themselves.

INTRODUCING A PREGNANT WOMAN TO HER COMMUNITY

The period after the fertility ritual and before the pregnancy is known as the time of the *spiritual pregnancy*. At least for Dagara people it is impossible for pregnancy to occur without the woman being *spiritually* pregnant first. In other words, the woman has to have heard the *call to pregnancy* or have left the door open for a soul to come through. Countless souls are always waiting to come through, and they do so only when we allow them to.

The spiritual pregnancy ends when the journey of the new soul in the womb of the mother begins. This new phase is an occasion to celebrate — and the mother-to-be and the incoming soul are joyfully introduced to the community and wished well on their journey.

Unfortunately, many people around the world describe pregnancy and birth as a nine-month medical condition, accident, or painful process, or they use other negative words rather than defining it as a positive experience. Pregnancy should be seen as the inauguration of an important person, a VIP stepping into a job that will bring much goodness to the world. We must celebrate this arrival and make it known to our community.

In the village we celebrate the arrival of the soul through ritual and celebration. A ritual space is created with shrines and all kinds of decorations. Food is cooked while the village sings. Elders take the mother-to-be into the shower room and give her a shower; then all the women come in to wash her. Then they dress her up, and introduce her and the incoming soul to the community, at which time all members of the community, one at a time, give their welcome to her and to the soul. They touch her stomach as they offer prayers and blessings to her and the baby, then they kiss her belly. We do this each time a woman becomes pregnant. While all this is happening, people sing and jump with joy. The song goes like this:

> *Ancestors, we heard a call and we answered it.*
> *Now our hearts are rejoicing. We thank you. And*
> *you who have come into our sister's home, we*
> *welcome you. You who have opened the door-*
> *way to the great mysteries, we honor you, we*
> *value you. Our hearts and hands are open to*
> *welcome you. Let us hold you. Let us make a safe*
> *space for you.*

A shrine is created for the baby during this ritual, mainly to facilitate communication between the parents and the child. The shrine usually starts with a gift of a medicine bag the grandparents bring to the ritual. Water, earth, plants, and fabrics are used to create the shrine. The shrine can also contain precious items that others at the ritual may have brought for the mother-to-be and the baby. Contents of the shrine and the medicine bag increase as the parents-to-be are guided to bring items the incoming soul will point out to them during the duration of the pregnancy. Parents-to-be often notice that certain things pull them like magnets. These are things that often point to the purpose of the incoming souls and need to be placed on the shrine. Later they can add elements the baby has indicated to the elders or during the hearing ritual (see next section). Food is also served daily at the shrine for the incoming baby and his or her friends from other dimensions. Thus, a shrine is, and will be, a sacred space that holds the baby's identity. Each time parents need to strengthen their bond with the baby or with each other, they can return to the shrine.

Bonding with the baby must be done daily throughout pregnancy. Each morning when the mother-to-be wakes up, she must check in with the baby by tuning into its energy. Not only is she expected to embody the baby's behavior, but also she is supposed to enact the baby's feeling, needs, and desires throughout her pregnancy. For instance, when a pregnant women craves for unusual food it is seen and understood that the baby is wanting those foods. If the mother is crying it means that the baby is emotional and these feelings come through the mother. Staying tuned into the baby's needs allows the elders to learn more about the incoming soul.

HEARING RITUAL

As mother-to-be and baby journey together through pregnancy, there comes a time when the elders do a life purpose check with the baby. This is done through what is called a "hearing ritual." It takes place a few months into the pregnancy.

For this ritual everybody wakes up in silence and no words are spoken before the invocation. The only means of communication allowed are gestures. Before dawn four women wake the mother-to-be with light strokes, and when she opens her eyes they tap her with some ash. (Ash symbolizes the element of fire, and fire enhances vision and the ability to connect with the ancestors.) The women help her get up, surround her, and walk her to the family's shrine room, which has been turned into a cavelike shrine for this occasion. Around the shrine is a stream of ash. The elders motion the mother-to-be to take off her top if she was wearing one. With her belly exposed, she is then carefully guided to lie on an earthlike bed surrounded by different kinds of stones, wood, bones, and bowls of water.

After a prayer invoking the ancestors and the spirits that dwell in the earth, woods, rivers, mountains, and rocks, everybody extends hands over the woman in support and blessings. Soft drumming emits sounds with an intention to crack open something hidden; the drumming guides people in a song of a *gate opening* and worlds meeting. Four gatekeepers stand in the four directions, each holding a stick and dressed in red, white, green, and black-blue, representing respectively the South, the West, the East, and the North. A fifth gatekeeper stands in the center, a few feet from the woman. All gatekeepers pound on the ground at the same time, and call their direction to open. The woman's mother kneels at her right side and the husband's mother at her left side. While they pray, the woman's mother traces a line of charcoal powder mixed with *shea* butter from the woman's diaphragm to her pubic bone. The husband's mother does the same from one rib cage to another, making sure the lines meet at the belly button. The woman's brother wards off any unwanted energy. The husband's sister from the father's side of the family (in Africa this is known as the child's female father) stands at the bottom end of the earth bed by her feet with a bowl of water and a bunch of *gomatín-gnobalu* leaves that she uses to mist her and the air.

As the singing intensifies, the woman enters into a trance-like state and her body soon gives into that of her baby. The song then becomes softer, and the elders get down on their knees to make sure the woman has become a channel for her baby to speak. After a long prayerful greeting, the elders tell the baby their intention. They then ask the child what it is coming here for — what its purpose is, and why it has come at this particular place and time. They ask what needs to be done to have a space that's conducive to that purpose. They listen very carefully, then set up the space accordingly, and a name is found.

A *divination* is always done to make sure that an agreeable name is chosen for the baby, for a name can be a blessing or a curse. A name is an energy that taps into the mystical dimension of a person. To know a person's name in the Dagara tribe is to have an access code to that person's world. If approved by the ancestors, the name is then kept secret until after birth when it becomes a reminder of the baby's purpose and identity. The ritual can also reveal the birthstone of the baby and other information about the incoming soul such as any particular food, animal, or fabric colors that could heighten or slow down the deliveries of the baby's gifts. These are carefully noted, and those beneficial to the baby are made prominent in the baby's life, while those that hinder in any way are avoided in the baby's life. If the mother heard the child's name before this ritual, it is possible to double check it at this time, and make sure it truly reflects the child's purpose and identity.

As the ritual ends, the woman regains her body and voice. She usually does not remember much about her experience, and often feels exhausted from the trancelike state. The ancestors are thanked and the ritual is closed.

BIRTH PROCESS AND ITS RITUAL

Before conception a midwife is always assigned to the mother-to-be. It is her job to supervise each step of the pregnancy, so by the time of the birth the midwife is attuned with the woman's energy and knows what awaits her. It is as though the midwife must become pregnant along with the woman. At the birthing, the woman and the baby must align their spirits to make the passage easier.

A few days before the anticipated birth, the midwife facilitates a few rituals. She prays to the spirit of all the midwives who have gone before her to get their blessings for the birth process. She asks the ancestors to make this birth as smooth as possible.

Birthing usually happens indoors, near the family's and the baby's shrines, except in some cases when the baby decides it wants to be born somewhere else. When the spirit of the baby starts to make its way to this plane of existence, the mother begins to feel turbulence, and so the welcoming committee, elders, and midwives take their place.

While they wait for the first sign of contractions, the women surround the mother-to-be and the men surround the father. The women, however, are the only ones who participate in the birth. A special birthing stool is usually brought for the woman in labor to sit on; otherwise, she just squats, and pulls on the other women's arms for support. The midwife puts some ash in the hands of the mother-to-be. As she labors everybody labors with her. The women do downward movements while they sing, "I feel a Spirit in my body. I feel it pressing, I feel it moving. There it comes, umm, I am letting it out." When the baby comes out he or she is immediately put on the mother's belly. Some of the first blood of labor is put in the mother's hand and also on the ancestral shrine. The baby's first cry is responded to with lots of enthusiasm.

WELCOMING OUR CHILDREN

Everybody loves being welcomed by joyous, enthusiastic, and happy faces when returning home from a long day of work or from a trip away from home. Being welcomed helps our psyches feel at home, and feel that we belong. People who have been to foreign lands where they did not speak the language will tell you what a difference one smiling face made for them. Being welcomed puts an end to our long journey. We don't want to go somewhere where we are unwelcome or threatened in some way.

This is as close as I can explain the process of birth for souls coming to Earth: Our children need to be joyfully welcomed when they are born.

Perhaps the Dagara's traditional African approach to welcoming a newborn may give other cultures another way to welcome children — and maybe even those of all ages who were never lovingly welcomed at birth. The Dagara believe that what happens to us at birth and while in the womb actually molds the rest of our lives. How did they come to have this practice? The answer may lie in the understanding of our personal gifts, and in the importance and significance of being welcomed.

Just like the preparation for pregnancy, the welcoming of the newborn is crucial. Indeed, in the Dagara tribe the first cry of the baby is critical. It is not seen as a simple cry, but as a coded message that is delivered upon arrival. In the village, children of up to five years of age are placed in the room next to the birthing room to answer the baby's first cry. They respond by crying back the way the baby cried, seen as answering the call and letting the newborn know it has arrived at the right place. At that time the baby then sends a signal back to the ancestors letting them know that it has arrived. After this initial dialog, everybody then sends out a welcome to the baby.

After the baby has been with the mother for a while, the children are asked to come, and the baby is then presented to them. One child will hold the baby while the others surround it in admiration. Children are close in age to newborns and remember their connection to the spirit world. Therefore, it makes sense that they would be the ones to welcome the newborn. The Dagara people believe that our wounds of abandonment start at this early stage of life, and so our welcoming of the newborn by children and the entire village at this early time in life is critical to the newborn's development.

Most people around the world don't think about the possibility of children being so highly sensitive and easily influenced at such an early stage of life, but they certainly are — even while they are in the womb. In fact, most think that when children are hurt they will not remember it when they grow up. On the contrary, children will store all the hurt and have a hard time healing later on in life unless these wounds are addressed earlier in life. If the first cries of the newborn are not responded to, the psyche interprets this to mean that no one is there for it. Therefore, an unanswered cry leads to a deep wounding of the soul and later will translate at the community level as anger or violence in some form.

We can bypass lots of ills in our world if we look at how we handle our children's births. We have nothing to lose and probably more to gain than we can imagine. Planning for a better future starts at birth — not ten years later.

AFTER THE BIRTH — THE PLACENTA RITUAL

When the baby comes out of the womb, while other people are celebrating, the midwives wait for the placenta to come out (if it did not follow immediately). Though long delays of the placenta after birth are rare, the birthing process is not over until the placenta comes out and has been placed inside a clay pot. In cases of delays the midwife often uses different techniques — gently stimulating the mother's nipple, applying pressure on her lower back, gently massaging from the stomach to the uterus, or using a technique I have seen my grandmother use: While sending out another prayer she moves her hands from the mother's vagina to the clay pot four times. At the end of the fourth time, the placenta follows her hands before she reaches the clay pot.

In most cases the umbilical cord is cut after the placenta is delivered. (There is a belief that by cutting the umbilical cord prior to the placenta being delivered there is a danger that part of the baby's soul will be left in the mother's womb.

Therefore, it is very important that the placenta be delivered.) The baby is passed over the placenta three times if it is a boy or four times if it is a girl. The numbers are important because the numbers are encoded with specific energy: three is energetically encoded with masculine energy and represents the sexual organs of man; and the number four is encoded with female energy and represents the sexual organs of woman.

After the welcoming ritual, mother and baby are brought near the baby's shrine and close to a fire that will be kept burning. The fire keeps alive the connection between this world and the ancestral world. A traditional giveaway to the ancestors is done immediately to thank them for the baby's safe journey.

After the mother's belly has been pressed with several warm cloths and hot water, her body is massaged with special plants mixed in *shea* butter to avoid her blood from clotting.

The newborn is sometimes not washed for three or four days, again depending on whether the child is a boy or a girl. But eventually both mother and baby are bathed in special plant medicines to strengthen, protect, and give them vitality as well as an abundance of milk.

While mother and baby rest, the women begin the placenta ritual. All women participate in it. The two grandmothers, along with the elders and midwives, guide the procession to the place where the placenta will be buried.

A hole for the placenta has been dug by a man in a very specific way: he keeps his feet together, so that they touch, throughout the digging. In this way, the hole is kept sacred and free from his energy. The hole is at least twice as deep as the size of the clay pot, or deep enough for the pot and a tree to be planted. The placenta is thanked for holding and caring for the baby in the womb. It is then offered to the ancestors to be blessed.

The new mother and the baby join the crowd and pay their respects to this life-giving organ if they are able. She first wash-es her feet into the hole. The hole is then thoroughly watered, the pot is placed inside, and on top of the pot a broken piece of another pot is placed. The grandmothers and the midwives put enough earth on top of the pot for a tree to be planted and still be able to receive nutrients from the placenta.

The earth is watered again and the tree is planted on top. The tree planting can be delayed if weather conditions are not favorable to its growth, and sometimes the placenta is buried under a large tree already established if conditions are impos-sible for a new tree to be planted. The tree is maintained by others until the child can take care of it. This spot becomes a place where the child goes to reconnect with his or her source, roots, and origins. If the child ever goes through a difficult time, the tree can be revisited for strength and courage.

Over the years this spot is where answers to some of life's

questions lie. This is why you may hear it said in many villages that someone is married to a tree. In the village, before people marry or before they have children, they must journey back to the tree, where they do a ritual with the tree to reconnect with their source.

The placenta ritual is done for each newborn. Today in Africa, especially in cities, the neon lights of the modern world, and the easy availability of holes that have already been dug have hampered the effect and diluted the importance of this ritual. But, even today, the city-dwellers know that an uncared-for placenta leaves both child and mother vulnerable and ungrounded.

NAMING RITUAL

A name is an important word with meaning and energy that identifies someone or something. Our names bring certain patterns to our lives and have the capacity to forge our destinies. A name is also used as a way of entering into a person's world, wisdom, or life. It's a code ingrained in us that allows us, when it is called, to remember, recognize, and respond to our purpose. This is why when someone calls us by a name that is not ours we do not respond to it. It is also why when someone attaches a negative name to us, such as "stupid," our whole being rejects it vehemently. Behind the word "stupid" is a weapon destined not only to disarm us but to wipe out whatever knowledge we may be carrying in us. So our reaction sends a message that is powerful enough to annihilate that energy.

Naming rituals are usually done after the critical bonding time between mother and baby. The baby is always touched and held close throughout the day, and sleeps body-to-body with the mother. First-time mothers leave the house only at night or if they are completely covered. Always having a person available gives the baby a solid foundation. It helps the baby know there are people here, people who are supportive. This continual bonding, which takes place primarily in the shrine room, reassures the baby it has arrived at the right place. It also takes away any feeling of abandonment and allows the baby to keep his or her gifts intact. This transition period usually lasts four weeks for a baby girl and three weeks for a baby boy. It is only after this time that the baby is slowly introduced to this world and to daylight.

⊷══◉═══⊱

We are all born with at least two names. The first name maps our life purpose; the second — our last name — states our connection to mystical dimensions: animal, mineral, botanical, and so on. For instance, my last name, "Somé," means Hare. The mythical understanding of the hare is that it is the messenger of god to people. It is also the tactful one and the mediator. You can see it when you read African stories. In the Dagara tribe, it is usually the mother's last name the children take. The first women ancestors made pacts with certain entities so that they could have access to their dimensions, be their allies, and be protected by them. So a name is sacred and must be treated as such.

The belief in many African traditions is that children go through several stages before becoming full human beings. They go from the stage of pure energy — spirit — to the stage of the spirit in the human body. After the welcoming ritual at birth, the naming ritual becomes the second step of introducing the baby to the human world.

The first time a child's name is announced to its community it must be presented in a sacred way. An anxious group of villagers waits outside while at the center of the ritual space are the elders and the grandparents. Until that day the baby's true name is not said out loud.

A libation is poured, calling the ancestors and all spirits. The parents walk in the center of the group holding the baby. After bowing, the mother hands over a girl baby to her mother-in-law; if it's a boy, the father hands him to his father. While walking close to the baby's parents, the grandparents introduce the baby to the different directions and elements, asking for protection, groundedness, clarity, strength, and nurturing. They also ask the spirits to ensure that the baby stays intact and is able to fulfill his or her mission.

The grandmother or grandfather whispers the baby's name three or four times, depending on the baby's sex, into the baby's ears. The name is then said out loud the same number of times. All members of the community whisper the name into the baby's ear, then give their blessings and hopes as they come down on their knees to speak to the baby.

The blood from the birth previously put on the shrine is brought out and brushed on a clay image of the child's totem animal. This reinstates the people's connection to the great mysteries. In the Dagara tribe, the understanding is that for each baby born a totem or protecting animal is born. People's lives are intimately lived and influenced by their totem animals, to the point where when a person's totem animal is hurt, that person can also be hurt. It dies only when the person it is protecting dies.

My first introduction to these animal realities happened through my grandmother's totem animal, for the animal loved showing up at all major intersections of my grandmother's life. Her totem was a small gray lizard called a *wouô*. When I was very young, I woke up one morning and found a lizard curled up around me. I was scared by it at first, and ran. My uncle came to look at it and then said it was Grandmother's spirit animal. It had a missing toe, just like Grandma, and a few other distinctive marks only the two of them shared.

In Africa your totem animal is your ally, your guardian, something you have a pact with. The family totem, a collective spirit guardian, protects the family as a whole. If I were pregnant, a crocodile would show up right near my husband's family shrine to alert his family of my pregnancy. The crocodile is my husband's family totem, with whom they have had a pact for centuries. Someone from his family will never drown because a crocodile will always prevent this from happening.

The baby is then named under the umbrella of his or her power animal except in some rare cases when the baby is having difficulties staying on Earth. This, the second naming, is called *Siou*. It is also known as a process of reawakening the spirit of the baby. The *Siou* name is not used as an everyday name and can be used only under certain circumstances, like in ritual space or when an elder wants to announce something serious. You know when this name is used that something important is about to happen. And you dare not let everybody know this name. The *Siou* name is also a diversion from outside forces that may play against the baby or keep the baby from achieving his or her purpose in life.

GRANDPARENTS AND BABY-BONDING RITUALS

Life is a ritual. It is full of mysteries and codes. The role of the grandparents is to reintroduce the baby to the myths, symbols, and mysteries of the world by keeping the baby's awareness alive through continual bonding. The relationship of the grandparent to the child, along with that of the community, helps diminish the trauma of growing up and keeps the child's gifts alive. It is their proximity and kinship to the world of the ancestors and spirit that makes children and grandparents special and unique — because the grandchild just arrived from that world and the grandparents are preparing to return. They each have the duty to inform the other of what's going on in their world.

Involvement of the grandparents in the child's life is essential for the child's well-being, and the well-being of the grandparents as well. Grandparents often act as the protector and the voice of their grandchildren. Many people around the world see the relationship between grandparents and grandchildren as trivial, therefore they think that the two get along simply because they have one enemy in common — the parents. Could this way of looking at the parent-child relationship be why children often have the worst time with their parents? The grandparent-grandchild relationship is important simply because without a good relationship between the very old and the very young, everyone else is left hanging, without an anchor. The nature of the relationship held by these two extremities in age is very healing and powerful. It has the capacity to take confusion away and to bring us close to one another. The news the grandchild brings from the ancestral land is useful for the whole village and finds a receptive ear, thanks to the grandparents' presence. And the grandparents' need of reassurance that the relationship with the ancestors is still intact is translated by the grandchild.

In the village the intimate relationship between the very young and the very old is kept alive by constant bonding and through rituals. Like any relationship it is subject to renewal.

The Dagara usually do simple yearly rituals. Grandparents sit in one row, and some 200 yards away children stand in one line. Each grandparent is paired with at least one child, and they sing the song of praise to the ancestors. (*Sâan minè* are male ancestors, *Mâa minè* are female ancestors.)

> *Puor-ah Sâan minè*
> *Puor-ah Sâan minè*
> *Puor-ah Sâan minè oooooh*
> *Puor-ah Sâan minè ooohhhhh Ahhhh*
> *Puor-ah Mâa minè*
> *Puor-ah Mâa minè*
> *Puor-ah Mâa minè oooooh*
> *Puor-ah Mâa minè ooohhhhh Ahhhh*

While singing, children at first walk toward grandparents; as the song picks up they start to run. The "Ahhhh" at the end of the song is when they fall into the laps of a grandparent. Then they start all over again and repeat several times.

Throughout the year grandparents and their grandchildren do what is called a "back bonding" ritual. They sit back-to-back, usually grandmother to granddaughter and grand- father to grandson, and allow their spine bones to protrude and touch each other's. In this way they are able to deeply communicate. They stay in a meditation posture for as long as needed. Sometimes they sing or tell each other stories. Bones in our culture represent memory; bones carry stories in them. When you sit with your spine touching another person's spine, it is like transferring information from one computer station to another.

I can see some people reading this and imagining it's a simple or easy thing to do. But nothing comes easy or without practice. You have to work at making this kind of relationship happen.

As a Westerner, if you find meaning and healing in this or any other ritual, you, too, can make it work for you. It may actually be an opportunity for healing, for letting go of old grudges so you can give to the children what they deserve most. And to this end I salute all grandparents and all grandchildren.

⤙⟞⬤⟝⤚

MISCARRIAGE

Regardless of culture, the loss of a baby is devastating. Miscarriage is often compared to lightning striking a tree at its core. It hits both the couple and the community in its most vulnerable place, putting the future of the village in jeopardy. It is a very draining experience that takes a toll on the couple and the community physically, emotionally, mentally, and spiritually.

THE DAGARA PHILOSOPHY OF MISCARRIAGE

The Dagara people's understanding of miscarriage lies in their knowledge of the universe and the interplay that exists between dimensions. It is a process that brings concrete evidence of mythical dimension. In the indigenous world of Africa, the term "miscarriage" is defined as a powerful and major event in life. It is the cancellation of a long-planned travel arrangement, leaving people at the destination heart broken and grief stricken. It is also a message from the spirit world, and a life-transforming experience.

From the African perspective miscarriage is a direct or

indirect intervention of god or some dimensional beings known as the *chièkuo* (chi-è-ku-o). The *chièkuo* are beings who travel the galaxy. They have been called the "travelers" or the "passing through" spirits. Strangely, they like the idea of going to a place, but they don't like staying in one place for any length of time. They have difficulties letting go of their worlds to come into this world, which is different from what they know. When a *chièkuo* decides to enter a womb, chances are the pregnancy will end in miscarriage, in a stillborn baby, or in sudden infant death syndrome (SIDS).

At the first sign of miscarriage, a divination is done to find its source. The divination brings insight to the miscarriage and can prevent future miscarriages.

A special ritual is often required to trick the *chièkuo* into staying among us. Though their actions are not appreciated, they are in fact child advocates — they are teachers who suddenly appear and usually bring specific messages. Their role is to call our attention to the importance of children and to remind us how susceptible and vulnerable we can be to losing our children. Though this message is sent through a couple or a family, it addresses the community at large. It usually alerts people to the importance of strengthening their relationships with their children and of creating protective forcefields around them.

In Africa people always keep an eye on the *chièkuo*. In fact, they will try to find out before conception if the village might be subject to these beings. They are not uncommon — I myself am a *chièkuo*. I am an example of how these beings can inter-fere with the birth process and how, with commitment from the community, they can be persuaded to stay. Somewhere in the depths of my being, I can still remember the times my mother was pregnant with me and had to miscarry simply because I was not here to stay. When I think about it now, I can't imagine the amount of pain she must have experienced.

My mother miscarried me twice. The third time she con-ceived me, she was able to carry the pregnancy to term and gave birth to a girl. I lived for six months. I was a fine baby. The day I decided I had had enough of this world, my mother said I had been sleeping, then I woke up and was playing and laughing. In fact, she says I was unusually happy. She watched me play, and then she turned to pick up something. When she looked back again I was lying down and silent. She reached to pick me up and could tell something was wrong. Indeed, some-thing was wrong: I was dead. And it all happened in one moment, just like that. In medical terms, this is called SIDS, but in village terms this is defined as a *chièkuo* who is returning home. Unfortunately, such a return home leaves the village in grief and turns life upside down for everyone.

When miscarriage happens to the same woman several times, a permanent distinctive mark, known as scarification, is put on the baby's body. After marking the body the elders say to the deceased baby, "The next time you come back to us, we will know who you are, we will recognize you, we will see it on your body." This way of handling the *chièkuo* has proven effective because when the same baby comes back, he or she will carry the healed mark put on the body before burial. Also, a special name is given to the child — especially if he comes immediately after the last incident.

I carry a mark on my body from my former life. When I was born again, some people present at my birth had also been present at the marking of my previous body. These people performed a recognition ritual acknowledging my return. They said, "We know who you are. We see the mark we put on you the last time. This game stops now! Now that we have you in our hands, you are not going anywhere."

This ritual does not guarantee that a *chièkuo* will not try again to slip away, but it gives the elders a chance to stay alert, keep their eyes on the baby, and work with the baby to facilitate a change in his or her pattern.

I continued to try to find ways to leave this world and return to the world I knew so well, but this time each attempt resulted in doors being shut to show the determination of my people to keep me here. Now that I am here, it is very bizarre to think about leaving. I was about six years old when I finally decided to put an end to the process of trying to leave. Although it was difficult for me to have to stay, my mother befriended me in a special way and made me promise to stay. It was a long and emotionally intense process that led to my staying here.

⊷═◉═⊶

Indigenous people believe there are other reasons for miscarriage, similar to the *chièkuo*, but for the most part miscarriage is a way for us to listen to the key spiritual truths being brought to us.

There are also theories of ancestors sending messengers to their former families to get their attention or to alert them to something. The messenger, who is actually an ancestor, comes in the form of a baby who is miscarried. For instance, upon leaving human form, the ancestor finds its human family in constant disagreement. The miscarriage then becomes a way for the ancestor to bridge the difficulties in its family and to make peace. Through the tragedy of miscarriage the family is brought together when they find the message of peace through divination.

Miscarriage can also be viewed as being self-initiated at certain times. Sometimes there are those who want to find ways to initiate contact with, or to break through to, another dimension. It starts with the willingness of the woman or the couple, whether consciously or unconsciously, to experience something deep, profound, and life-altering. An agreement is made with beings from the other side to experience something of unknown design that will open her to the mysteries of the universe.

Another example of the source of miscarriage is attributed to God — or gods — who gives life and takes life away.

GRIEVING THE LOSS THROUGH RITUAL

Because there are so many reasons for miscarriage, a family sends a *diviner* to find out the exact source of its pain. But no matter what the diviner finds to be the core source of the miscarriage, the community must deal with its loss and grief. It is amazing how much grief both men and women carry in the face of a miscarriage or the loss of a child. Grief has the capacity to go beyond gender, culture, and race. We may think that things are happening just to us, but the truth is that our grief and pain are not isolated. When I see an American woman who miscarried in grief and pain, it may well have been any woman in the world. And indeed the best and most traditional response to miscarriage is grief because no amount of justification will take the pain away and no amount of reasoning will bring the baby back to the womb.

Grieving is a soul-cleansing ritual. It has an energy capable of cleaning away lingering clouds and festering wounds in one's life. Over the centuries it is one of the ways Dagara people have used to make peace. While a woman is miscarrying, she is surrounded by other women of the village who not only support her, but witness and go through the experience with her. After she miscarries, depending on her state of health, a full grieving ritual takes place that allows her to go through the pain of her loss with her community. This is an intense grieving ritual that lasts 72 hours. Usually, this experience is so draining that it takes all her energy and leaves her nothing to do but rest. If she is too weak to partake of such an activity, a more moderate version allows her to deal with the loss without losing herself in the midst of it. In this case people come to her sickbed and hear her tell her story as they grieve together. The presence of other people supports, witnesses, and affirms the pain of a sister who has been chosen as the vessel for a message that addresses the whole community.

I remember when my aunt miscarried and we participated in her ritual. At that time she spoke some words that stayed with me. After the opening prayer, she was asked to share her experience. She said that her heart and soul were being watered by the presence of all her loved ones, that she did not have much strength to share, but that she had a few words to share with the spirit who had left her belly. She then began:

> *Spirit of my Ancestors, Spirit of the Kontombile,*
> *Spirit of the* chièkuo *and of the mysterious world.*
> *It is to you I am calling, it is you I am talking to.*
> *I have seen much pain, I have lived through the*
> *unthinkable, but what happened to me today was*
> *not something I awaited. I wished it not on me,*
> *not on anybody. How come you let me down, my*
> *mothers, why did you forsake me, my fathers? I*
> *feel betrayed and unworthy. The spirit I awaited*
> *left me in a vortex of grief, anger, sadness. And*
> *without a good-bye, my home is wrecked, my*
> *spirit in great turmoil....*

Before everyone knew it, we were all grieving. My aunt's speech sent a shock wave through the room that brought her pain and grief to our already fragmented hearts. From then on the grieving process took its own course. At the center of the room was a clay pot were the blood of the miscarriage was collected before the ritual began. Things that reminded people of the pregnancy were also put in the pot with a prayer.

Toward the end of the ritual, gifts were put in the pot along with the blood, just as you might send some presents home with a dear friend who came to visit you. The only difference is that with this ritual you require of the deceased baby certain things. For instance, someone may say, "I give you this gift. On your next trip back I need you to commit to staying so we can grow together and let our spirits bloom together." Someone else may phrase this differently, but the important thing is to tell the miscarried baby that miscarriage and grieving are not at all fun to be going through and you want it to stop now. You must reiterate to the spirit the significance of its being here. When you voice your concerns it makes the spirit realize that it has to be cautious and that it can't just use the body of this woman to go back and forth between dimensions.

After everyone has spoken, the clay pot is sealed with leaves and buried. When the woman recuperates, during the next full grieving ritual, her miscarriage pain and grief are added to the ritual and the whole village joins her to mourn her loss.

THE HEALING PROCESS

I share these stories because I know there are many people who have experienced miscarriage and who are trying to discover what it means and find a way to alleviate their pain. Healing the emotional wounds of a miscarriage certainly does not mean hiding your pain, pretending it never happened, or minimizing it in any way. Most people, including Africans, think that not showing emotions is a sign of strength. But how can we be strong when we keep our feelings inside, and don't express them and, ultimately, heal them? It could very well be that our lack of expressing our grief is the cause of many illnesses we experience. Maybe it is the lack of a validating community that keeps us from grieving and ultimately healing. One thing is for sure: Our psyches will remind us of our lack of acknowledgment during this time of crisis. For those people who are in touch with their emotions, the challenge is to overcome the influence of a society that says it is not okay to cry and does not validate their experience. It is important to know that your tears are not wasted, but that they heal your wounds. This was a baby, a baby that was part of a dream. Every tear is worthy and worthwhile.

Miscarriage is a life-transforming experience. If it never happened to you or to someone close to you, this may be an altogether foreign concept. If you have had a miscarriage, you are certainly not alone if you felt completely alienated by the experience. Most people in contemporary societies find it hard to relate to, or have feelings for, something they cannot touch or see. The most difficult thing about pain is that it is invisible. What we see on the surface in terms of external injury is only the tip of the iceberg. Miscarriage is one of the places where the physical damage does not reflect the truth because, in early miscarriage, the only proof is the bleeding, but the immensity of the pain is without words. For the miscarrying woman, life will never be the same because she has experienced something completely different from the normal, waking reality: She has broken into the mystery of the unknown and the invisible world, and she inevitably comes out of it with a stamp on her soul.

In societies where individuals are left to figure things out by themselves, some people may choose simply not to deal with their grief because they don't have a context for it, a corpse to mourn over, or the support of their communities. So they don't even allow themselves to acknowledge the miscarriage as a loss. Most often the grieving process is not even considered, and any emotion or thought about the miscarriage is quickly dismissed. The grief will not go away, however, because we hide it somewhere deep within our bodies. On the contrary, it will go deep into our cells. When this repressed grief gets into our very inner being, it leads to physical illness. In spite of the cultural conflict around grief, acknowledging your loss in a cathartic grieving session will save you years of therapy and possibly even life-threatening illness later in life.

From the Dagara perspective, everything that happens in life happens for a reason. There is no victim, there is no coincidence, and there is definitely a gift behind each of our experiences. So you have to look at the gift and at the wisdom that the miscarriage brought.

The truth is, however, when miscarriage happens it is often very hard to find the gift because our pain and suffering are the first emotions we experience. When we give ourselves the chance to deal with the grief, pain, and confusion, we then start to see that there is a gift hidden behind the wound. For some people it may be a wake-up call, a call to reconnect with soul and spirit, a rearticulation of purpose, a need to see and acknowledge what they have already been gifted with: an experience of the unknown, having experienced death at the core of their being and surviving it, or simply a recognition of the need for a community to come together and to experience life together again.

For my mother, it took several miscarriages before she came to terms with a promise she had made as a child after losing her mother. Though she had many mothers who cared for her like their own children, she promised herself to give birth to her own mother. She had a need to create that special person she knew only for a short time. Though she came to understand she could not produce her mother herself, the gift she received was that she found her mother hidden in all people — children as well as adults, essentially the mother in all — and it helped her to reevaluate her relationship with others and to cut her ties with something unhealthy that caused her much pain. But ultimately, the miscarriages and the healing that came from them brought such a gift, such a transforming energy into her life, that it completely changed things for her — life was meaningful once again.

The long and painful experience helped my mother learn to let go and to forgive — to forgive her mother for leaving her and to forgive herself for feeling responsible for her mother's death. She also realized that her mother literally gave of herself so her children may live.

⊷═◉═⊷

It seems to me that in many countries when a woman of modern society miscarries, the involvement of the community is almost insignificant. The experience then lacks validation, and the gift that comes out of it, the wisdom that comes, is often not discovered and therefore not valued. Without acknowledgment, the experience leaves the woman and her family empty handed, without anything palpable.

People say, "Don't worry, you can have another child. This was just a passing experience, don't let it bother you." As a result, the psyche interprets this experience as completely invaluable. If it isn't valuable, if there was no reason for it, the woman so often comes to feel that, in some way, she must have done something to cause it to happen. Many people struggle and feel guilty, because guilt is so readily available, instead of seeing the gift in front of them, as my mother was finally able to see.

It is important to feel from the heart — to go through the grieving process. Then we can truly begin to heal.

❖

CHILDREN

In Africa it is understood that children hold the knowledge and gifts that ensure the survival of the village and the tribe. In essence, the child is the king of the village. When a child walks into the middle of a crowd, all attention goes to him or her as if to applaud an arrival long awaited.

Children complete the community! Without children, the world is a dead end and communities would not exist. Children are the life-givers, the healers, the messengers of the ancestors. They bring out the spirit of the community — they bring spirit home. Children are embraced, celebrated, and supported, for without them there would be emptiness in the hearts of all villagers.

A child is valuable and irreplaceable, someone we cannot afford to lose. The world has embraced the truth that childhood shapes the women and men we are today. Because of this realization and deeper understanding, we have the ability to put a stop to destructive generational patterns and raise our sons and daughters with respect, self-esteem, and true commitment to their lives.

In the Dagara tribe, we know we cannot have community without children, we cannot have children without community, and neither would exist without spirit. It is one complete circle, each element completing the whole. We welcome our children and in so doing we welcome spirit.

Because the health of the community is intertwined with the strength and health of our children, we must encourage our young to develop healthy, positive awareness of the self. This is why we start the process of discovering a child's identity long before its birth.

A CHILD'S NAME AND IDENTITY

As discussed in the chapter on birth, children in our village know their identity and their life purpose before their birth. Throughout children's lives, the community continues to reinforce their identity, which helps them tremendously to know who they are and to remember their purpose. Our identity and purpose are intimately tied together and encapsulated in our name.

For example, my name, Sobonfu, means "she who keeps the rituals of the ancestors alive" or "she who brings back the lost rituals of the village." I "chose" my purpose because many people in Africa today are walking away from the traditions of their ancestors. Many are sidetracked; they don't live out their purpose, and their lives are unfulfilled. It is my purpose to keep the rituals alive so that the cycle is not broken. Every time a person uses my name, I am reminded of my purpose.

Most people do not understand the power in the meaning of names. And many people struggle with not really knowing who they are, making it difficult for anyone else to *really* know anyone else. People will have their own judgment of who we may be; however, 99 percent of the time they are completely wrong because they are seeing only a small part of us — the surface — and they miss the part of us at the core. They make their own assumptions that what they see is who we are. And what eventually happens is that we start to believe that what people think of us is truly who we are. That's how powerful the energy behind our thoughts is.

The question is, Can we live with some of the assumptions people make of us? Often we accept what people think of us as reality. The worst part is that we make it okay for people not only to treat us that way, but also to treat our children the same way — until one day something inside says "no more." Then the struggle for our true identity and the craving for others to see our true self begins.

When you are brought up without a community to support you, chances are you will use whatever form of community you can find. You will draw from individuals around you in the hope of creating a community without even knowing that it is community you are wanting.

We all want to belong to something greater than us. We want to feel loved, needed, valued, and respected, and often children will turn to various groups around them looking for a sense of community — a sense of belonging. In this situation, however, they never know who they are dealing with or who holds — and who doesn't hold — their best interests at heart. They are likely to become involved with people who will bring them the toughest lessons of their lives.

Imagine being a child under these circumstances, in a culture where there is no true sense of community. Imagine if everyone thought of you as dumb or ugly, and that's all you heard every day. Imagine the kind of energy and meaning these words carry and what kind of impact they would have on you. Eventually these energies will create an umbrella — a home under which you live — and slowly they become your reality. It is only logical that a child being called dumb begins to act dumb unless something is done about it.

When children live in non-supportive environments, they are subject to judgments and assumptions from friends, teachers, peers, and often even their own parents. It's often difficult in the world today to protect our children from these problems.

This is why community is so very important. Caregivers and those wanting to build a solid foundation for children can create a forcefield around them so they are not completely damaged by the experience of name calling and other negativity. They can use words and take actions to build, heal, and edify, showing children that there are positive ways for them to build a strong sense of self and identity.

If substantial damage has already been made, there is a

need for healing. Because our hurts are such an important part of our learning experience, we must learn to use the hurt as an antidote, a healing medicine that helps us to move forward rather than an experience that shuts us down. We must learn to use the experience as a special kind of food — food that is meant to give us strength, ambition, motivation, and courage to continue our purpose. If as adults and parents we can bring this understanding into our children's lives and create a ritual whereby they can flush the negative elements out of their lives and begin with a brand new eye and renewed determination, then we will have accomplished something not just for them, not just for our families, but for the greater good of all.

Suppose your name is Jim and everybody calls you "Junior" or some other nickname that makes you feel insignificant or maybe even, in some way, almost invisible. This name, with its connotation of smallness, will affect your life and identity in many ways as you grow into adulthood — and, your great gifts become invisible or meaningless. In the African tradition of the Dagara people, to heal from his invisibility Jim would be taken through a ritual by which he would be made visible. The ritual would start by speaking about the feelings of smallness or nothingness and how it has affected his life. The same way words damage us, we can undo the damage by speaking about them in a ritual.

The same ritual can be done in the West. A supportive community determined to end the invisibility or low self-esteem in Jim's life would listen and respond with affirmations and encouragements. When Jim finishes the ritual of speaking his hurts, he can symbolize the negative attachment to his name in the form of a picture or some similar thing that he can burn. Jim could go on a journey to a shrine made of elements of nature and fire where he would burn this symbol along with all the feelings that came with it. He would then go to a water shrine where he would be cleansed both energetically and physically with water and leaves.

A name affirmation would take place: Jim would stand in the middle of the community and tell his true name. The name would be repeated back to him by all attending his ritual, and to all the spirits and the directions as well. Then each person would whisper the name into his ear and, finally, they would all say his name together out loud, just as in the naming ritual of a newborn. In this case, his name is Jim — not Jimmy or Junior. Small nuances in a name make a big difference. As the community affirms and validates his true name, it is also validating his gifts, purpose, and experience. Effort must then be made daily to reinforce Jim's identity.

NURTURING A CHILD'S ABILITIES

Children heal faster than adults and are able to start life on a new footing as soon as we make the effort to stop inflicting them with negativity and give them the opportunity to heal. If we continue to ignore the fact that our children are the greatest gifts to our world, then we should consider ourselves an endangered species. If we can think of our children as priceless, however, then it will be easy for us to focus on their positive side and offer them the love and respect they deserve.

⋆⇒◉⇐⋆

Often we focus on the reality of the family, without letting our children know there are other realities out there also. It's important to notice the other realities, without judgment, and to know that it's okay to draw from them if they are useful. The reality of the home is one thing — the reality of the world, however, is another. Give your child a way to start to monitor the world.

Children are endowed with an incredible memory and ability to learn. They watch their entourage with an eagle eye, with curiosity and precision. They naturally intuit what is needed and can draw from their environment to emphasize their gifts and develop their character and will.

We often think of children as being complicated; however, children's realities are very simple. One thing is sure: children respond to genuine love, not the kind of love that comes encoded with conditions, or any kind of agendas or demands. Our children need to know that we are there for them and that, no matter what, they can count on us. They need to know that they are held dearly in our hearts. Always tell your children that they are needed, they are okay as they are, and they are good inside — especially during adolescence, which is a time of anonymity, loneliness, and a time when nobody fits in and when the world seems to be sending the message, "Nobody is out there for me." By being a mentor and actively validating your children's identity, you can and will strengthen their core being. Instead of thinking of themselves as dumb or incapable, they will understand that they are worthy and worthwhile, that they have a purpose, and that their lives have meaning. Only then will they start to feel that the world has meaning, also.

A CHILD'S VOICE

Children need a voice and a listening ear. In the village, because everyone is your father and your mother, you feel that you can count on all the villagers and that you can trust them. When many people are parents to a child, it makes it possible for the child to go to anybody and just sit and talk. Everybody in the village knows what is happening in all the children's lives — there are no secrets. The village is there to be their ear, to hear their voice, and to encourage them to speak their truth.

If children don't have an outlet — a chance to be heard — they will keep their voice inside along with their gifts. If we don't encourage our children to talk and be open, they learn other ways to let their voice out, and this energy can become highly destructive to them. When children speak it liberates them. It lets the toxins out, and new energy can come through. But when they don't speak, their thoughts, emotions, and experiences stay inside and can eventually pollute their lives.

When I first came to the United States, I experienced this truth firsthand. I was used to saying things instead of holding them in. In my village people are always receptive and available at all times. When I came to a foreign country and didn't have people around, and, worse, when I couldn't speak the language and had to rely on my husband for translation, I felt constrained and awful. Most of the time I had no choice but to hold it in, even though it was against my very nature. Without even being aware of it at first, I was slowly dying a painful death. I noticed that simple things came blasting out of me, because they were jailed inside of me and were becoming toxic. With time I learned to find new and different ways of expressing myself, I found new people to talk with, and I discovered the great value of learning this new language. I also learned how to create community wherever I went, and to sing as I used to in the village so my spirit did not die. Having a listening ear allows for an incredible peace to come in, for both the speaker and the one who listens.

We can do the same thing with our children that we need to do for ourselves — we can learn to be patient, not judge their every word, encourage them to let go of negative things, and not turn their hearts and souls into storage places for junk. It is possible for children to find and keep their voice instead of having to seek it later in life after an emotional bomb has gone off for them. Simple things such as singing, dancing, art, and music are great ways of liberating the child's spirit and voice. But the most important thing is to encourage your child to speak, and to listen.

Years ago I lived for a summer in a small city in California. Our neighbor had a daughter, and every day when she came home from summer school she would take off her backpack and tell her parents, "I am going to Sobonfu's." In the beginning her mother said, "No, don't go. Don't bother her, she is probably busy." "I don't care," the girl would say, "I'm going anyway." And she would come and I would sit and listen while she told me elaborate stories. And when she was done she would get up and say, "Okay, bye," and go back home. As time passed I talked with her mother, and without betraying the girl's confidence or trust I let her know what was happening in her daughter's life, and strongly suggested that she pay more attention to her. I never gave particulars, but the mother was able to put her attention where it was needed.

As it turned out, the young girl did not feel welcome in her family, and it was excruciatingly painful for her. She found comfort in talking to me. And because the mother and father were going through their own pain, they had no time to allocate to their daughter, and so they did not see her pain, and certainly had no understanding of her feelings and behavior. It was difficult for them to stop what they were doing long enough to see her pain. But when they did, it brought about healing for the whole family.

By reaching out to me, this young girl created an extended family for herself. She began to put together her community —

her group of people that supported and loved her. Community is a natural thing — if we don't have community in our lives, we often create it.

We can create extended family and community by opening to our neighbors, family members, co-workers, and friends. Then when children need to be heard by an adult, they can be heard, regardless of blood relations. It is through this sense of community that the child's voice is heard and brought to the attention of the parents and the community. There is nothing wrong in asking for help from other people because we are not able to provide something for our child. There is, however, something wrong if we are too proud to ask for help. Had it not been for the trust this young girl put in me and my lack of judgment of her, she probably would not have been given the opportunity to be heard. Eventually, she accepted some input from me, but being heard and being able to express her feelings and thoughts was her goal. After she accomplished her goal, healing began.

It is not enough for children to be willing to share their experiences or for parents to give permission for children to share their experiences. It takes effort on the part of all involved to make the healing process work. This is what is meant, at its core, by community. The unified involvement of a community of well-intentioned people allows a child to weave together relationships of family and friends that broaden the child's worldview and knowledge. When this happens, you know that the attempt to create some form of community has helped the child and will allow the child to feel support-ed, loved, encouraged, and safe.

This is how children in my village learn their irreplaceable value in the community and the importance of the community for their well-being. This is why no child is truly an orphan in my village, because there will always be at least one mother or father to take care of this soul, even if the biological parents are absent. All people caring for the child do so with all their hearts, souls, and love in order to give more than what the bio-logical parents may have given.

Children are seen not only as spirits coming to give their gifts to this world, but also as spirits who are here to test our willingness, our generosity, and our genuineness. What do we have to lose by giving our best to our children? I believe the gain is far greater than what we can even imagine. Let's remember that each second counts in our interaction with our children. Let's not kill their spirit or their imagination in any way, for to encourage our children's creativity and voice is to allow our children to blossom.

Children are like containers inside of which all kinds of goodness and craziness happen. In order for their goodness to emerge they sometimes go through the swirling blender of craziness. But it is the presence and guidance of adults, espe-cially elders, that help change the crazy ingredients into some-thing nourishing and soul enlivening. We must be careful as adults not to negate, intimidate, or stifle the creativity of their imagination and their voice.

I remember when my grandmother would ask us children to share in creating a ritual. She would provide us only with the purpose and intention of the ritual — the rest was up to us to figure out. Sometimes, we came up with something marvelous; other times we did not. Grandma did not immediately jump in and say that the ideas that were not so good were not valid, nor did she negate our experience. What she did instead was to let us know it was good and that we needed to take into account certain things the next time we created a ritual. Or, she would ask us what we would like to change or what kind of ingredient we would add to bring more strength or meaning if we were to create this ritual again.

In working with children this way, we start to notice the kinds of gifts they have. As we spend time with them and allow their creativity to flow through, we start to see the gifts that are unique to them — gifts that nobody else has. And, as we see their gifts, so do they. This is part of their identity of self, and their life purpose begins to emerge.

To allow children to express themselves, to be heard and to create, is to call forward their spirits and to open their world and other dimensions to us. Allow the expression of their voice, and embrace it — and be open to the gifts it brings.

A CHILD'S SENSE OF SELF

Often, we tend to look at other people without actually seeing them — we notice only what serves us or affects us in some way. When it comes to children, our ability to notice and see must be magnified. The smallest detail matters.

We have all heard, in recent years, that we have within us what many refer to as our *inner child*. A lot of us suffer a great deal in our lives because our inner child has old wounds that have never been healed. It is important to know how to overcome our old wounds, because all too often they stand in the way of our ability to fully love ourselves, other people, and the children in our lives.

Our old wounds often become our children's burden. Many adults lack patience when children are present, and this impatience can be magnified when the children are receiving attention from others. We must begin to take steps toward our own healing. I can share a ritual that enables us to begin our healing process.

One way to heal the wounded child within is to practice giving the love and attention that you may not have received as a child to your own child or other children. Giving a child attention does not mean inflating a child's ego with a false sense of self. By giving love to children and by nurturing the spirit in children in a true and unselfish way, we actually heal our own wounds. It sounds so simple, but it does work. It happens almost miraculously, because what you put out comes back to you.

For example, I know a young girl who had been raised by her father and stepmother for the first part of her life and has just recently moved into her mother's home. Her mother is a friend of mine, and she confided to me that at times she becomes very cold to her daughter and pushes her away, especially if she feels lied to or betrayed by her in any way. They are in family therapy together, and both the girl and mother are focusing on the inner child.

Recently the mother experienced a revelation as the two were quarreling. Instead of closing down and pushing away, she consciously chose to open herself and listen to her daughter, and to remember how she felt when she was 12 years old, to remember the powerful emotions running through her. She remembered what it was like to be pushed away by her own mother and treated as if she didn't matter. When she felt this she made the conscious choice to stop — she made the choice at that moment not to pass the hurt onto her daughter.

As she did this she found that she was able to resist her usual coldness and stand-offishness with her daughter and to reach out to her. And the daughter felt the openness of her mother and shared more in those few moments than she had in the previous eight months. It was a very healing process for both of them. The mother actually felt her inner child being taken care of while she was opening up to take care of her daughter.

That evening the mother made the decision to stay open to her daughter, and not shut down again. In so doing she stopped passing on the hurt from her generation to the next and began to feel forgiveness toward her mother, for this hurt had been passed through her.

This kind of situation provides great opportunity for parents who are having difficulties being present with their children to get into a ritual space, for there is an urgent need to stop this ongoing wounding. Involving our children in rituals allows them to open up so they can speak their truth without putting on a mask.

I'm not suggesting that one healing ritual will solve all problems. It takes commitment from all involved. But it is a beginning.

Many people would say this process can be done without a ritual or a community. The difficulty with problems settled outside of a sacred space is that our human tendency wants us to always be the one who is right. Our courtroom-style mentality forces us to pick one person to be the scapegoat for all that goes wrong, and healing never takes place under these circumstances. A ritual space allows us to be honest and less defensive. It lets us look at the crisis not as an occasion to beat one another up, but as a message from spirit to renew our relationship, or take our relationship to its next step. Although a ritual is not like a pill you can swallow once and for all, its continual use keeps us on a steady, healing path.

Simplicity is the key to making things happen. Keep your rituals simple and clear. It helps to open invisible doors we may not know are there. It takes the opening of such doors for children to come from the heart and speak heart to heart with their peers and people around them. Again, the key to this is for the parent not to jump to quick conclusions or judgments that will shut down the child, but to remain open to receiving the emerging identity of the child.

It is natural for children to not always be eager to listen to their parents, of their many layers of emotion and feeling between them. But the same thing a parent may say can be said by friends or aunts and it is well taken because of their openness and lack of judgment. In the village there are other members of the community who can provide this help.

An open-minded conversation and a nonjudgmental attitude gives children the freedom to express themselves without feeling that the world is going to come after them. It gives solid layers of foundation to children so they know they can walk on this foundation without falling. Having their feet in two worlds — the home and the community, family relationships and friend relationships, the earth and spirit — helps with the process of children discovering their true sense of self.

A CHILD'S COMMUNITY WITH OTHERS

It is natural for children to want to be in a community with others, whether the community is comprised of adults or children. The child's sense of self is held by the community. Their spirits and sense of self blossom in community. What we sometimes find is that the best caregivers of children are children themselves.

You see it in the village from the way children interact with one another — the love that one child has for another cannot be substituted by anything. No amount of toys or electronic games can replace the love from a child. Children have to be around other children because there are things they say to one another that adults cannot say. There are different energies children give one another to strengthen their sense of self that adults cannot give. They express friendship, love, mentorship, and spirit. For this reason alone, in my village a family with only one child will ask that another child come and stay with them to create the child-to-child dynamic.

This relationship is not only taken seriously but is also respected in the village. Whenever children have spent a certain amount of time with one another and it is time for them to go their separate ways, we must do a ritual to temporarily separate them. We always leave something of the departing child with the other child and vice versa, so that each child knows the bonding energy is still there. This is so critical today, when so many families are torn apart through divorce and children are separated from one another. The children may or may not show signs of great distress right away, but later they will know they have lost an important ally.

You can see a special energy when you put two children together. Before you know it, they have figured out a way of connecting with each other. This shows especially when you take a child to a foreign country. The adult may be still confused, trying to find his or her way around, but a child will be with other children, learn the language very quickly, and fit in right away. I sometimes think children have some kind of homing device that allows them to recognize one another. The elders say that children speak a language among themselves called the *chièkuo* language, which allows them to communicate without adults interfering. It is the same word used for the travelers or passing spirits. Only here, it is the language used, not the traveling.

When I was about five years old, I was always taking care of some children, and I remember when my younger sister was born. I was her ally and she was mine. When someone wanted to pick her up and it was obviously not the right time for her to leave my company, she wouldn't go. She would hang on to me and scream until the other person let go. When it was time for her to go, she would peacefully go to another person. She had found in me the kind of energy she needed, was taking advantage of it, and was not willing to let go of it until she was satisfied.

Young children don't have to talk to communicate with one another. Even if they are together without talking or interacting much, the child will still cry if you try to interrupt the communion. Usually it's a matter of timing. It is best to wait until there is a closure — when the children move away from each other on their own — before you separate the children.

This kind of communion is valued because the wisdom children share with one another is a kind of wisdom adults have forgotten. Children are fresh messengers from Spirit. They bring news on matters that pertain to our well-being. This is why elders and grandparents take their relationships with children so seriously — children have messages for us that the elders have to decode.

Children, along with elders and grandparents, create a stable environment for adults to live in and to carry out their purpose. Elders and children form the backbone of a community, a fertile ground upon which many wondrous things can be grown. A society that rejects their elders will eventually reject their youth and will find itself going crazy as a result, for there cannot be a balanced society without children and the elders.

You can tell if the relationship between the very young and the very old is taking place by the amount of strength and groundedness that exists in the society.

⟶⟦◉⟧⟵

To help children grow and come into their true being, we need to look at them differently instead of always looking at them from above. We need to simply come down on our knees and talk to them. Think for a second what it was like for you looking at all those grownups talking to you from way up there — how intimidating it was. The gap between adults and children is huge in most Western countries. We can attempt to make it smaller or even bridge it by changing our attitudes and our ways of relating to our children. We need to address them not as possessions or things, but as wise people, spirits who have something to share. It makes a huge difference in their perception of themselves as contributing human beings.

When children value themselves as human beings with gifts, then they can give to the community, and to the world, and can fully participate in the greater good.

SUPPORTING A CHILD'S SENSE OF WORTH

In the village they say our best teachers are children. No child is born without a purpose. We come to this planet because we have something to give to the world. The elders in my village are always working with children to protect the children's purpose. As adults, we may close our eyes to certain things, but children do not, and when they speak they speak the truth.

Imagine the strength in speaking the truth without fear. It is such a liberating act to speak what is in your belly. I can still hear my grandmother encouraging us to speak our truth in these words: "Speak it and liberate your heart and mouth." The point is that truth is encoded in us and the way we speak it is unique to each of us. There were unique circumstances that led to our birth in a particular village or town or to a particular parent, and our truth is spoken in unique ways through our walk, talk, grief, and smiles. Continuing to keep our children speaking their truth in the modern world is a continuous challenge we must face every day.

Far too often we put a few people in the spotlight — movie stars, singers, presidents — giving the illusion that to be like these people, to look like them and to act like them, is to be good, perfect, and right. Our children interpret this on a subconscious level, feeling that if — and only if — they are like those people they see in the media, then they, too, are somebody. It is a terrible message for children.

There are so many extraordinary people who have many great things to say and to contribute, and nobody pays much attention to them simply because they are not in the spotlight. We must protect our children from falling into this self-defeating trap by repeatedly reinforcing their sense of worth and purpose. It is essential for children to know they are unique — and to know that being unique does not mean putting others down, for everyone else has their unique gifts as well. We must also reinforce the idea that their sense of purpose should not be closely linked to any other person — celebrity or not — and that within their sense of worth and unique purpose is their true identity, and it needs to be nurtured and cultivated.

Children struggle because they find doors shut before they even grow out of infancy. They rebel because they don't know how to make people hear them. We have children turning to gangs because they feel all the other doors are shut, and a gang offers the kind of relationship that comes close to what children would have had in the community. In the gang, the members support one another much like a community does. These children feel that the gang is better than nothing. The danger here is that once they get into a gang they can't get out.

The pressure of modern life is everywhere in the world. In

some African villages, including mine, our youth are also rebelling — not against the community, but rather by welcoming the pressure of the modern world and the invasion of the media. Their way of rebelling is to go to the city. Their view of modern society is that everybody has everything under control, and people don't have to do much to get what they want. Unfortunately, their city experiences are often frustrating and painful. Sometimes the city has death waiting for them. Despite the elders' warnings, they go to the city in the same way they go to other villages, thinking that people will be there to hold and support them if they begin to fall. They go to the city and live in conditions that are different from and foreign to the villages, and then they are exposed to all kinds of emotional and physical diseases.

Just like the many African cities that are lost in the pursuit of the modern, many indigenous cultures will have to lose everything — or nearly everything — before they know that what they had was invaluable. Although steps are being taken in many parts of the world to conserve the valuable wisdom and way of life of the indigenous people, much more is still to be done. When I walk in some villages, I get goose bumps when I pass houses that are now abandoned and empty. I can't help but think about the amount of suffering and grief that must have been there. It brings tears to my eyes and heart knowing that the absence of the youth have left some women to die of broken hearts and left the elders purposeless. A village without its youth is a dead village. The elders' wisdom is meaningless and the village life is without future. The pride of the village has been stripped away and its purpose has vanished.

No country has ever been able to survive without children. Robots and toys cannot replace them. Maybe we won't realize how valuable they are until there are no longer children. While there is still time, let them know that being here is in itself valuable. When your children learn that being born is a victory in itself, they will look at life differently.

A CHILD'S PURPOSE

We can learn many things from our children as they grow up that will expose what their purpose truly is. Children are constantly sending out messages; if a community listens and watches children carefully, it will see pieces of their purpose emerge. Obviously, children will be attracted to certain things. Pay attention to those small things children like to do; encourage the gifts they have and watch them blossom.

We cannot afford to go to sleep at night unless we know that our children feel safe, worthy, wanted, and worthwhile. We must protect them. We must encourage them to come forward and to stay in their purpose. We must fight for their well-being and their gifts.

When I am in the company of children I am always reminded of a fight between a crocodile and a mother pig I witnessed at the village river. The mother pig was taking her babies to the river bed to have their daily wash. As the piglets were enjoying themselves, the mother went in search of a deeper water hole, while still keeping an eye on her babies. A hungry crocodile grabbed one of the piglets; crocodiles use the bodies of small animals as bait to catch fish. The mother rushed after it, and chased it down to the deep hole the crocodile had made for itself. After a long and bloody fight the mother came back safely with her baby. She carefully licked it, and then gathered all her babies out of the water and arranged them around the one the crocodile had tried to get.

After I saw this scene I said to myself, this is something to die for — to die for the well-being of children. Just like the mother pig protected her baby, we must protect our children. If they are our future and if we acknowledge that they have a purpose, a gift to give to the world, can we afford to lose them or to pass on to them our old multigenerational wounds?

⋆⇒◉⇐⋆

I believe it is time to take a stand for family values that are essential to our well-being, values that honor and respect our children, elders, and community. It is time to loosen our grasp on individualism and greed, and to go back to a time where children are life and life is children, and where each child was the child of the whole. It is time to come together in community to support and protect our children and to find our own unique ways to welcome Spirit home.

MAKING RITUALS WORK FOR YOU

Most of the rituals described in this book are not complicated. Their simplicity and vitality can inspire even the most ritually-impaired person to create and apply ritual into daily life. If you have found the rituals described in this book difficult to apply to your life, these suggestions can help you adapt them to your lifestyle. Although most rituals call for the presence of a community, you will see how easy it is to make them fit your particular situation. These rituals have proven very successful in the West.

The biggest obstacle for most people is overcoming their fear of failure. There is not just one way of doing any ritual. The truth is, if your heart is sincere, your intentions are for the greatest good, and your ego and sense of control disengaged, then all you need is respect for the traditions from which you are drawing and a willingness to dive into the unknown with the blessings of spirit. A ritual need not be fancy or complicated, and it must never be ego driven. What makes a ritual work is its simplicity and the clarity with which it is done.

Before we move into specific rituals there are a series of steps that may need explanation to help you understand their symbolic meaning. These important steps should always be followed: bathing, the initial prayer, creating a sacred space, and the closing prayer.

BATHING

Many African rituals either begin or end with bathing. Bathing symbolizes washing away old habits and old wounds. It is a way to renew one's spirit — a way of taking a new step, of embodying healing energy and moving from one stage to another. It also symbolizes rebirth and a state of purity.

THE INITIAL PRAYER

The first step in any ritual is the initial prayer, which sets the intention and purpose of the ritual. Your initial prayer must be clear, uncomplicated, and specific. It is a way to invite your spirit guides to help you reconnect and remember key elements of the ritual that allow you to heal and connect with the self, the natural forces around you, and community. It must come from the belly and the heart, and often it is done by the community on behalf of the people for whom the ritual is being performed.

CREATING A SACRED SPACE

A sacred space embodies healing energy and holds together the energy of the ritual. It is a place of beauty and a place where spirit and the ancestors dwell. Creating a sacred space is a collective activity.

In creating a sacred space, you may or may not need to use all the five elements: fire, water, earth, nature, and mineral. It depends on the ritual being performed and your specific need. If you are unable to locate any of the five elements, you can use a colored candle to bring the vibration of a particular element into your sacred space. Choosing a colored candle that fits the purpose of the ritual you are about to do is important because the energy from each colored candle will be different. For clarity, I've put together a quick reference list (see page 114) indicating the color of the candle, what element it represents, and the vibrational energy it promotes.

Here is a list of other tools you can use when creating a sacred space using the different elements:

- *Water*, in a blue bowl if possible. The blue bowl also represents the color of water.
- A bowl of fruit and/or a bowl of soil to represent the *earth* element.
- A small potted plant, flower, or twig to represent *nature*.
- *Mineral* can be represented by bones, stones, and metals.
- For *fire*, you can use a mask. Masks represent something old, ancient, including the ancestors. You can also use ash, which is the remnant of fire, or even better, fire itself.

- You may also use other items when creating your sacred space that have special meaning to you, such as rings, clothes, pictures, or some other personal object.

Candle Color	Element Represented	Vibrational Energy
Blue or Black	Water	Promotes peace, reconciliation, and focus
Red	Fire	Enhances vision, the ability to communicate with the ancestors, and dreams
White	Mineral	Facilitates memory, remembering, and a connection to people
Green	Nature	Allows for easy transitions and magic to take place
Yellow	Earth	Creates a grounded energy, sense of identity, and fertility

THE CLOSING PRAYER

When closing a ritual it is necessary to thank the spiritual guides and the ancestors for their guidance in showing you obstacles that you could not see and for bringing healing. You also want to thank anybody who has joined you in your healing journey.

CHILDREN AND RITUAL

Children are by nature ritually alert. As they grow up, their environment can take them away from their ability to relate to ritual. The best way to teach children how to incorporate ritual into their lives is to expose them to ritual. Oftentimes, we discover something that works for us and want the same thing for our children. We can be so insistent with our children that it almost becomes an opposing or imprisoning energy for them. The same thing can happen with rituals. If this happens, children will stay away from rituals rather than embracing them. Be careful not to force your children to participate in ritual. Allow them to be part of ritual to the extent of their capacity. This way, they won't feel that they are under pressure to perform or to be in a place where they do not want to be. If they are forced, they will start to have resentful feelings, and resentful feelings would create an energy that repels the very thing you are wanting to work on. Let them do as much or as little of the ritual as they want. In this way, ritual becomes natural to them.

While children's participation in rituals is important, understanding the meaning behind a ritual and the symbols is critically just as important. When children are ritually taken through the different stages of life, they will understand the meaning and strength behind rituals, and feel supported in their journey through life.

STORYTELLING AS A RITUAL

There is a mythical and a ritual dimension to all stories. Many rituals have been kept alive through stories. The simple fact of telling stories takes us into a ritual where we commune with the divine. In my village, there is a prayer made at the beginning of each story session to open the gates where stories are kept, to open the gate to the divine. Storytelling is a communal event. In my village, there are days when the elders tell stories, and on other days, the children tell stories. Sometimes the children start the story and the elders finish it or vice versa. By telling stories in this way, everybody is heard. This is valuable because when a story is told, you can tell what is happening in the life of the person telling it, and it points out what kind of ritual is needed for that person. And telling a story to a group, family, or community can bring everyone together.

DREAMS AS RITUAL

Dreaming is one of the places where we dive into rituals without resistance. We can use our dreams to do healing rituals for ourselves or for other people. Again, you need to use and focus your intention, to ask for guidance and answers with an initial prayer before going to sleep, and to be willing to receive the information you are seeking.

Often, dreams send us valuable messages without our asking. Pay attention to your dreams — they just might be trying to tell you which ritual took place and which one is yet to happen, or simply tell you things you need to keep your eyes on.

There is no question that we all, at times, don't remember our dreams. This happens when we are agitated, frustrated, ungrounded, defensive, resistant to the work being done in our dreams, or when we do not find value in dreaming.

If you awaken abruptly before things can be solved in your dreams, you can carry the nervousness or anger from the dream into your waking hours. Try to wake up slowly and roll back to the side you were dreaming on. Lay down a few minutes and think about your dream. Keep a dream journal by your bed and write in it as soon as you wake up. You will be surprised at how much you remember and how much work you did during your sleep.

⟶⟨⟨⟶

Be creative, and always remember that rituals are serious and should be taken earnestly. Most people practice some form of ritual in their lives without thinking about it. When you celebrate a birthday, graduation, or marriage, you can turn them into meaningful rituals by bringing spirit, intention, and purpose to them. Think about the joy you receive when participating in a friend's or family member's birthday, graduation, or wedding. You can experience the same sense of joy, healing, and connectedness by incorporating rituals into your daily life.

Let's now take a look at specific rituals. Most of the rituals we will be addressing here are rituals that were discussed in previous chapters that celebrate healing, children, and community. They have been altered slightly to facilitate the modern world.

◦►═◉═◄◦

HEALING OLD WOUNDS

Many of us suffer continuously from old wounds we carry. Healing old wounds is an important part of life — it frees us to live life more fully and joyfully. An old wound can be feelings of abandonment you had when you were a child, or feelings of not being worthy. In both cases, your life will be affected with much pain and suffering unless you heal these wounds. An old wound can cause difficulty between you and a partner, with a child, or with other people in your life.

In the chapter on children, I spoke about my friend who was having difficulties communicating with her daughter — how she was able to overcome the urge to shut down, and how she opened up and really listened to what her daughter was trying to say. She was able to take care of herself as well as her daughter by allowing her feelings and her daughter's feelings to come through.

My friend has deep wounds — feelings of being inadequate. She grew up in many different homes and felt that her voice was not worthy of being heard. She never felt she belonged anywhere or meant anything to anyone. It is these old wounds that she burdens her daughter with. I have recommended to her that she and her daughter do a healing ritual in which they will be held by their community of friends and family.

If you too are in a similar situation, and if you want to begin a healing ritual, ask family members, friends, or neighbors to join you — people you know will support your healing. Upon their arrival explain to them the situation at heart. By asking family and friends to join you, you are creating a community for yourself. The community then prepares a sacred space by creating a shrine dedicated to peace and reconciliation, preferably near a large body of water — if not, a simple bowl of water would do. While your community is preparing the sacred space, take a walk to see if you can find things to symbolize your wounds.

An initial prayer then takes place as members of the community call upon the water spirit, natural forces, and the ancestors to come hold the space in such a way that healing takes place. In the case of my friend, she went to the shrine and spoke from her heart, in a non-blaming way, how hurt she has been by her own wounds, by lack of attention to her inner child, and by her feelings of worthlessness. These wounds prevent her from being able to be receptive to her daughter's pain.

She let herself experience her anger and rage. At first she felt timid and small, but as the community supported her in her pain she found the strength and courage to continue. She dared to speak from her heart and let spirit know, in front of her daughter, about all her feelings of frustration and vulnerability. This opened the doorway for her daughter to ask for help from spirit, and to speak her own truths in a non-accusatory manner.

The community participated by listening and supporting both the daughter and my friend in speaking their truth. It brought them both closer together, and they were able to focus on the peace that they were both searching for. The symbol representing the wound was burnt in a big fire. My friend and her daughter then stepped into a body of water outside their home where they each forgave themselves first, and then forgave each other. They were bathed by the community to wash away the old wounds and pains. Then they were both welcomed back into their new state of being with embraces.

The ritual closed with a simple thank you to spirit, the ancestors, and the natural forces. Over the next few days the community kept in close contact with them to ensure that healing was indeed taking place.

Doing this ritual will not magically dissolve all issues that may arise between the parent and child. It will, however, open the doors of awareness, honesty, and communication between them. It may be necessary to repeat the ritual until core issues are resolved.

If you discover during your healing journey that there are energies that you need to bring back into your life — such as mothering, nurturing, fathering, protection — you can incorporate rituals on a regular basis if necessary, with people that can help bring these energies into your life. For example, if you need mothering or nurturing brought into your life, ask a sister or aunt — someone you feel a nurturing energy from — to your healing ritual. In addition, you might want to take symbols representing memories that are not useful to you any more, such as an unhappy picture of you as a child, and either burn them or take them to a river or the ocean and give them away.

PRECONCEPTION RITUAL

In today's society hardly any attention is given to preconception rituals, yet the importance of these practices needs to be acknowledged. A preconception ritual should be the community's wedding gift to the couple. In this manner, the community brings their support to the couple while the couple affirms their dedication to the coming child. To create such a sense of community for yourself, invite friends, family, and neighbors to support you and to participate in a preconception ritual. One way to drum up a supportive community is by placing a book at your wedding ritual for people to sign up for a preconception blessing.

For this ritual, I suggest a journey back to your place of birth. If you can't go back to the actual place where you were born, use pictures from your childhood, toys, some earth, a stone from your place of birth, or some other object with symbolic meaning, to create a sacred place. This will also encourage your memories. If you don't have pictures, ask your parents questions about your birth and the places you lived in as a child — take notes and place them in your sacred space. You might also try painting a picture of your childhood home, neighborhood, or anything else that might refresh your memory.

In creating your sacred space, use all of the five elements: fire, water, earth, nature, and mineral. You will want to burn a candle of each color, with an accent on mineral candles. You will need a dish of water in a blue bowl, if possible, a piece of nature, an element from the earth, a lot of mineral elements, and ash for the fire element. It would be a good idea to use pictures of ancestors also for the fire element if you can locate any of them. (Refer to the list on page 114 for items representing each element.)

Begin your ritual with the initial prayer, which sets the intention and the purpose of the ritual. Journey back to childhood memories during this ritual, highlighting the things you lacked as a child and the things you gained. By doing this, you can be sure to instill positive experiences for the child you wish to bring into your life.

Once you have created your sacred space — your shrine — allow yourself to come in contact with the mineral element, the bones and stones. Pick them up, place them on your bodies, hold them — and journey back to the time when you were a child, or even further back, when you were in your mother's womb, to reconnect with those memories.

You *will* experience memories. Once you have, you need to allow healing to come through. This can be a challenge, especially if your old wounds have been incorporated into your life in such a way that they have become part of your identity. For example, if one of your wounds was covered up by alcoholism, you might be identified as an alcoholic. Even if you gave up drinking, you will still be identified as a recovered alcoholic. In order to move past identifying yourself with your wounds, you need to forgive — yourself first, for the wound your soul has suffered, and then those who have participated in the wounds. Ask for forgiveness in a prayer. Take turns and don't rush.

If you find it difficult to allow the healing to come through, look closely at the difficulty — where you're feeling stuck. Let yourself feel your anger, sadness, rage, and grief. When you have done this, you can then come to a place where forgiveness is possible.

The next step is to come into contact with the very energy or thing you did not have that created the wound. For example, if as a child you did not feel nurtured within the home and your home felt as if it was destroyed, you need to reconnect with mothering, nurturing energy. This should be done with community members present, a close friend, mentor, sister, aunt — anyone from whom you currently receive nurturing energy.

To know where you have been and to make the commitment not to create the same kind of energy in your future child's life — and to allow yourself to draw from the place of not having to a place where you can give everything you did not receive — is to truly take a giant step toward healing.

Healing continues as you make an effort to stay conscious of your wounds, not to rehash them over and over, but to make a conscious choice not to pass them to your children. This is done through prayer, through seeing a gift in the wound while holding on to the vision of healing. All of your community members should be praying and holding the vision for you as well.

In concluding this ritual, thank the spirits and ancestors for their help and guidance. Also, thank anyone that has joined you in your journey.

Note: You can also do a "shamanic journey" to go back to your childhood. You can, for instance, have stones or pictures from your place of birth placed on your head, chest, stomach, and in both hands while laying down to journey back to your early childhood to the sound of a drum beat. In doing this, you will encourage childhood memories and you will notice what you gained or lost as a child. By doing this as a couple, you can make a conscious effort to change things for your future child.

The journey to the place of birth and the healing ritual can be done in two segments or it can be combined, as in the case of the shamanic journey. Going on the journey to your place of birth and creating the space automatically begins the healing.

BONDING FOR A STRONG PARENTAL RELATIONSHIP

The ritual of bonding for a strong parental relationship allows a couple to renew their vows and remember the spirit that brought them together by going back to that spirit and asking that it continue to strengthen their relationship, to help them continue to fulfill their purpose, and to make space for the baby to come.

This can be done simply in a sacred space that you have created with family and friends that you wish to share with as you re-acknowledge your commitment as a bonded and loving couple. Have your friends dress you and bring you out while your community is singing for you. If you don't have friends and family close by, you can take a trip to the place you went on your honeymoon to reconnect and renew your vows to one another. In your sacred space, collect all of the elements and have a red and a blue candle burning to enhance focus and facilitate communicating with the ancestors. Your community will begin your ritual with the initial prayer, stating your intention. Reaffirm your commitment with each other, and close the ritual with a prayer, thanking spirit and anyone who has participated in this ritual with you.

Rituals do not have to be complicated — just clear and direct.

CLEARING THE WOMB FROM POSSIBLE TOXIC ENERGY

To do this ritual, I suggest using a sauna or sweat lodge. Put together a sacred space that your family and friends can hold for you while you use the sauna or sweat lodge. Begin your ritual with the initial prayer and then enter the sweat lodge or sauna. During this ritual, you want to let go of the need to hold onto something: your desire to have a child of a particular gender or look, any negative thoughts you have about motherhood, and anything that makes you feel uncomfortable or controlling regarding children and motherhood. By doing this you will help release any toxic energy in your body and spirit.

Use a combination of sage and lavender oils to brush and massage your the entire body. Drinking sage tea with a sprig of lavender in moderate quantity can be useful during this time. Sage and lavender are known for their healing abilities. After the sauna or sweat lodge you could also be bathed in warm water with lavender oil and epson salt to draw toxic energy out of your physical body. Consult the directions on the bottle of the oils to be sure you are using them properly. Using red and blue candles while bathing is also helpful — red representing fire, enhancing vision and the ability to communicate with the ancestors; blue representing water, promoting peace, reconciliation, and focus. You can do this ritual several times if you need to, but you must stop before doing a fertility ritual.

Close your ritual with a prayer, thanking the spirits and the ancestors as well as all who participated.

FERTILITY RITUAL

It is best if you can do this ritual in a cave, because a cave symbolizes the womb. There are many caves in the United

States that are accessible. If you cannot go to a cave, create one by putting up a tent in the woods, making sure that the floor of the tent is the ground and not a plastic liner.

During the initial prayer of the fertility ritual, the community should do an invocation on behalf of the couple inviting forces of fertility and calling upon a willing soul to come into the life of the couple. In its prayer the community should ask the male and the female energies to come together to produce balance and invoke fertility. The couple then states their reason for wanting a child and asks for the blessing of the divine.

To connect with the earth, you can create an earth bed in the cave or tent and lay down in silence for a good length of time. The earth bed does not have to be large; a simple rise of about one foot above the ground will do. While you lay down, the people around should be praying on your behalf — asking for a spirit to use your womb. In your prayer, state the commitment of you and your loved one and the community to care for the incoming soul.

Spend the night in your cave if you can. Your family and friends who have joined you in your ritual should try to stay to support and hold your prayers. At the end of the ritual, water is sprinkled on the couple to bless their fertility, as water is symbolic of life. Again, I would suggest using all different colored candles for this ritual, but more yellow candles (earth, for creating a grounded energy and fertility) and blue candles (water, for promoting peace, reconciliation, and focus).

This ritual will facilitate the spiritual pregnancy, leaving the door open for a soul to come through. The spiritual pregnancy ends with the beginning of the journey of the new soul into the womb of his or her mother.

When concluding your ritual thank the spirits and ancestors.

Note: After the fertility ritual, relax. If you have trouble relaxing, do relaxation movements or meditate to remain calm and peaceful. Drink a lot of water or herbal tea. A massage would also be a good idea.

⟶⟩◉⟨⟵

ANNOUNCING THE PREGNANCY

Create your sacred space with a shrine for the baby in your home. The shrine usually starts with a gift from the grandparents in the form of a medicine bag. The bag usually contains healing plants or a protective talisman. You can ask your parents, a friend, or future godparents of the child to provide you with one of these medicine bags. Things such as water, earth, flowers, potted plants, and your favorite fabric are used to create the shrine. The shrine can also contain precious items that participants at the ritual may have brought for the mother and the baby. The shrine and medicine bag will grow as you are guided to bring different items that you intuitively find or that the child points out during the duration of the pregnancy.

As always, begin your ritual with the initial prayer. The mother-to-be should take a shower in a room with lighted blue, white, and green candles (symbolizing peace, communication, and magic energy). After the shower she should be dressed up in a new white dress. The women who have come to be a part of the celebration introduce her and her newly conceived child to the rest of the family and friends who have gathered. All members touch the belly of the mother-to-be as they offer their prayers and blessings to the baby and the mother. Then they kiss her belly. Incorporate song in this ritual — songs of joy that everybody can sing along to. Then enjoy a pot luck feast with all present. Everyone who participates in this ritual will be a part of the child's life and community.

At this ritual, friends and family can commit to doing something for the child — becoming a godmother or godfather, being a mentor to the child, and so on. Close the ritual after the feast by thanking spirit and all members who attended your announcement ritual.

Have a book for people to write their blessings and where the parents-to-be can keep track of the stages of pregnancy — different feelings that arise, as well as communication between parents and baby while it is still in the womb. You can read the blessings in the book to the baby while it is still in the womb.

Later, when the book is completed, it can be one of the story-books you read to the baby after birth. This storybook will dif-fer from other storybooks that you buy because it is all about the child.

❖⸺◉⸺❖

The mother needs to bond with her child on a daily basis throughout her pregnancy. Each morning when she awakens she should check in with her baby by tuning into its energy. Staying tuned in to the baby's needs allows the mother to learn more about her coming child. As the mother learns more she can add items to the medicine bag. The father can do this along with the mother.

THE HEARING RITUAL

Hearing rituals can be difficult, but not impossible, for Westerners. During your initial prayer, ask spirit to allow you to "hear" from your baby. Ask that your baby tell you something about her or him so you can get an idea of what their life pur-pose is. After your initial prayer, all participants should medi-tate with the mother so she's able to relax. This helps her make her body and voice available to the baby. A group of family and close friends can encircle the mother-to-be and journey with her and the child while touching the expectant mother's body. Ask a close relative to hold the mother's lower belly with sand in their hands (a mineral to help with communication). The mother will journey with the child while the community holds the sacred space and vision, and helps the mother's will to not override the conversation, so they can hear the baby speak to them through her. At the end of the meditation the community comes up with a consensus of what they heard.

As you close your ritual, thank the spirits, as well as everyone who has attended. The hearing ritual can be done many times throughout the pregnancy.

Now that you have initiated a "hearing," pay attention to your dreams and look for symbols and patterns that show up in your life before pregnancy, during pregnancy, and after the birth. They can reveal a lot about your child's purpose. Pay attention to the different and unusual foods you seem to be adding to your diet. These foods can show you something about the child, if you open up to the possibility, and pray to understand the meaning of the different foods.

Pay attention to animals that show up that you would not see under normal circumstances, and to other things you are drawn to as well. All of these things are ways of hearing from your baby who he or she is. Try to find meaning in things that come your way.

BIRTHING RITUAL AND WELCOMING

Because today most people have their babies in hospitals, I recommend that the birthing and welcoming rituals be combined. Many people already do some form of this ritual. A few days before the anticipated birth, go to the baby's shrine that you have created in your home and do the initial prayer. Ask spirit for a safe and easy delivery. And then prepare your birthing bag. Inside your bag, bring something from your baby's medicine bag. Also bring some beautiful soothing music such as sounds from nature, the ocean, and children. Organize your friends and family and have some of them bring you food, run errands, provide massages, and assist you in any way you need. Have as many people in the room as you are comfortable with to encourage and support you on this journey.

More and more hospitals are now offering birthing chairs. If possible, ask for one. It is a much easier way of birthing than laying down on your back. If you can afford it, see if it is possible to try a home birth. If not, ask that the light in the hospital be dimmed as much as possible.

As soon as the baby is born, have the baby placed on your stomach — immediately, before the umbilical cord is cut. Then wipe the blood from the baby. When the baby first cries, all in the room should respond with enthusiasm. If possible, have children — or children's voices recorded — crying back so the newborn child can hear them. Also record voices of absent relatives welcoming the child over and over.

End the birthing and welcoming with a grateful and thankful prayer to spirit and all members of your community for holding your vision. A red candle should burn for approximately a month after the birth, or if it is winter and you have a fireplace, keep the fire going. This keeps the connection and the ability to communicate with spirit open.

Note: If the delivery of the placenta is delayed, stimulate the mother's breasts or gently massage her stomach. Before going into labor insist on taking your placenta home so you have it for the after birth ritual. Hold the baby a lot and sleep with the baby if possible.

AFTER THE BIRTH — BURYING THE PLACENTA

The ritual of burying the placenta has been done in the West for several decades now. It is becoming more and more popular as many people feel the strong spiritual benefit it embodies.

In most hospitals you can request to keep your placenta. You can keep it in a container in your freezer until you are ready to bury it — but remember to thaw it before burial.

Begin your ritual with the initial prayer. Ask as many women friends and relatives to attend as possible. This will be the foundation of your child's community.

Ask a close male friend to dig a hole in your yard or the yard of a relative if you don't have a yard yourself. Be sure it is a yard that your child can have easy access to. You might also consider digging a hole near an existing tree in a park. The hole should be deep enough to hold a ceramic clay pot (fired but not glazed), some soil, and a new tree. Place the placenta in the ceramic clay pot.

As you and your community gather at the hole, pass the baby over the placenta three times if it is a boy and four times if it is a girl. Ask spirit and the ancestors to guide and protect your child. Place the pot in the hole, and plant the tree on top of it. As you finish your ritual, thank the ancestors and everyone who has come to be part of your child's community in the closing prayer. This tree will become a place where your child can reconnect with his or her spirit. It will become a place that the child can go for strength and wisdom.

As with all joyous occasions, you could finish this ritual with a feast, song, and dance.

NAMING RITUAL

Before you name your child, I suggest that you research any name you are considering. This can be done over the internet or through one of many books. Talk to your parents — ask them where your last name came from and also what it means. It is always good to research the root of the name. Doing this gives you the full meaning of the name in your language or in your ancestors' tradition.

Sometimes a baby will reveal to the mother its name while she is taking a walk, or it will come in a dream, or during daily bonding time. It is a matter of listening and paying attention. Whether you received the name during the hearing ritual or at another time, take it to the child's shrine and ask for confirmation. Try to make it match the child's purpose. You will get confirmation in the form of a "knowing," a dream, or a vision. When you have decided on a name gather your community to celebrate the naming.

Begin your naming ritual with a prayer, stating your intention to name your child with a healthy, supportive name. If you pick a name and its meaning contains something negative, make sure you say out loud that this negative part is not part of the name you are giving your child; also say out loud that you are referring to the positive side of the name. For example, the name Mary means bitter in some traditions. The word *bitter* is not necessarily negative, but you would want to state out loud that your intention to use this name is for the positive energies the name embodies, such as a healing tree that heals with its bitter sap.

As mentioned in the birthing chapter, after the welcoming ritual at birth, the naming ritual becomes the second step of introducing the baby to the human world. The first time a child's name is announced to its community it must be presented in a sacred way. Have your community of friends and family stand in a circle. Select a person to represent and hold the elements of each direction. You can pour a libation or simply call the ancestors and all spirits. The parents walk in the center of the group holding the baby. After bowing, the mother hands over a girl baby to her mother-in-law; if it's a boy, the father hands him to his father. If your parents are unavailable to be present, pick someone of your choice that is close to you. While walking close to the baby's parents, the grandparents introduce the baby to the different directions and elements, and then ask for protection, groundedness, clarity, strength, and nurturing. They also ask the spirits to ensure that the baby stays healthy and is able to fulfill his or her mission.

The grandmother or grandfather whispers the baby's name three or four times, depending on the baby's sex, into the baby's ears. The name is then said out loud the same number of times. All members of the community whisper the name into the baby's ear, then give their blessings and hopes to the baby.

When closing the ritual, thank the community, the spirit, and the ancestors for their commitment to the baby. This is a very joyous occasion. You can end the ritual with a feast where everyone brings something to eat from their own ethnic background.

MISCARRIAGE GRIEVING RITUAL

Grieving is a way of cleansing the soul — it has an energy capable of washing away lingering clouds and festering wounds in one's life. Having a miscarriage is undoubtedly a very difficult time for the woman, as well as for her partner, close relatives, and friends. Support for the couple is extremely important. When a couple experiences a miscarriage one of them should alert someone within their community and put them in charge of immediately alerting the rest of their community. People should come to support the couple, and never try to make them minimize their loss or brush it away. Everyone must be willing to dive into the grief with the couple and support them at any given time.

Although the couple, especially the woman, might be in a place where they would like to isolate themselves, it is important to share the story of the miscarriage and let their community support them. People can share their own experience without taking away from the couple.

If the woman is too weak to partake in the activity of a ritual, those closest to her should come to her bed and hear her tell her story and grieve with her. The presence of other people supports, witnesses, and affirms the pain she suffers. This allows all people participating to receive a message from this miscarriage and grieving ritual.

When creating the sacred space, include many red candles to enhance the ability to communicate with the ancestors. Also burn blue candles to facilitate peace and reconciliation. Place a clay pot (not glazed) in the center of the room, and begin this ritual with the initial prayer. Be very specific in your prayer; let spirit and the ancestors know that you are grieving and need help getting through this challenge. After the prayer, gently ask the woman to tell the story of her miscarriage, her pain, and her grief.

Each person can put things in the clay pot that remind them of the pregnancy. The purpose for doing this is to send these gifts to the soul that has left the mother's womb. During the ritual remember to require certain things from the miscarried baby such as a commitment to stay next time, or to stop interfering, or any other commitment you might want to ask the baby.

The grieving process will take its own course. This is not intended to be an intellectual discussion of the miscarriage, and it can't be rushed if you want to get to a place of healing. A mother who has miscarried needs a lot of nurturing from her community. After everyone has spoken, seal the clay pot and bury it. Close the ritual in prayer. Thank spirit and the ancestors for their participation.

GRANDPARENTS' BONDING RITUAL

It is important for children to develop strong relationships with their grandparents right away. It's up to the grandparents to begin this relationship and for the parents to reach out to their parents to start the relationship with the newborn. One way to proceed with the bonding process is for the grandparents to make a date with their grandchild — to spend a lot of time together, some nights on the same bed, and to learn to listen to their grandchildren's story. As mentioned before, storytelling is an important form of ritual. Grandparents can tell grandchildren what it was like when they were young, and share their knowledge of the world. And children can pass on information to their grandparents about where they have just come from.

Another ritual that grandparents may want to adopt is the "back-bonding" ritual described in the birth chapter. Start your ritual with an opening prayer. Light red and white candles to enhance vision and the ability to communicate. Sit with your spines together and tell each other stories. Make the stories fun, with powerful lessons. Listen carefully to the child's stories and let them know how interested you are in what they are saying. Close the ritual with another prayer. Thank your grandchild for sharing with you. Before leaving, make another date with your grandchild to do something special together, even if it's a simple walk in the park.

CREATING A SENSE OF COMMUNITY FOR CHILDREN

Incorporating rituals into your life and the lives of your children will certainly help create a sense of community for you and your family. It is also good to keep a strong connection to all the people who have been present and have dedicated themselves to the child since before conception. These people form a community for your child. Another way to create a sense of community is to organize a gathering for your children with friends and family members who also have children. Take turns gathering at each other's homes. The family hosting the gathering can serve food from their ethnic background while the other families can bring food as well. This way your child can bond with other children and share what is necessary among them. It will also give children a sense of extended family. Allow children to reach out to other people in their lives to get mothering, fathering, or whatever they need.

Allow children to communicate among themselves for a time at the beginning of the gathering. Once the meal starts, however, incorporate the adults with the children. Children love eating in community. Talk with the children about what their day has been like and share your day with them.

The simple act of gathering together for a meal in this way is, in fact, a ritual of its own. What makes it so is the intention behind the gathering. Next time you and your friends gather together for a summer barbeque or winter celebration, begin your gathering with an initial prayer, keep a candle burning, and really communicate with those who have gathered. Allow yourself to share in a genuine and sincere way. Your children will see this and learn by example.

If your children see you with your family and friends in this way, they will know that they too are safe to be themselves.

Above all, remember that your children are the greatest gifts the world can receive. Treat them as such. They need and deserve our guidance, love, compassion, understanding, examples, encouragement, and trust.

⋆⇒◎⇐⋆

The fact that we are able to bring children into this world does not mean that we will always be equipped with what it takes to raise a child. It is not enough to want to be a good parent; we need help and community — it takes community to keep a couple sane. The fact that children have people around them does not automatically give them community. It takes a lot of work, commitment, and our intention to create community. Rituals will not make themselves happen in our life, we need to *make* them happen.

If a child grows up with the idea that only mom and dad are her community, then when she has a problem, if the parents cannot fix it, the child doesn't have anybody else to turn to. The parents alone are responsible for whoever the child becomes, and this is too much to ask of just two people — or, many times, just one person.

Giving a child a broader sense of community helps him or her to not rely on one person and helps prevent feelings of isolation. Then the child can go to a person of his or her choice.

Take a stand for your family's well-being. Honor and respect your children, elders, and community. It is time to come together in community to support and protect our children and to find our own unique ways to welcome Spirit home.

May the divine mother and father remain alive in you.

⟿══◉◉══⟾

ABOUT THE AUTHOR

Sobonfu Somé was born and raised in Burkina Faso, the former Upper Volta, and is an initiated member of the Dagara tribe of West Africa. Her voice was one of the first to bring African spirituality to the West. She continually travels the world conducting seminars and workshops that offer her perspective on birth, pregnancy, community, healing, intimacy, rituals, and the sacredness of everyday life. She is the founder of Ancestors Wisdom Spring, and her previous book was *The Spirit of Intimacy: Ancient Teachings in the Ways of Relationships*.

Sobonfu and Malidoma Somé are giving back to the village by working on an ongoing project to provide water to the Dagara villages of Burkina Faso. Financial contributions and other sevices help these efforts to continue. Drilling equipment, pumps, and other materials are needed. If you would like information about the Somés' workshops and seminars, or about the Friends of the Dagara Water Project, please contact:

Echoes of the Ancestors
P.O. Box 4918
Oakland, CA 94605-6918
Web site: www.PrimaSounds.com/echoes/